101 Simple Service Projects Kids Can Do

BY Susan L. Lingo

Standard
PUBLISHING

CINCINNATI, OHIO

DEDICATION

Whoever serves me must follow me; and where I am,
my servant also will be. My Father will honor
the one who serves me.
John 12:26

Special thanks to Barbara Bierd, Kathy Duggan, Lisa Flinn, and Nanette Goings for their lively ideas and suggestions, their servants' hearts, and their love of kids. God bless you!

101 Simple Service Projects Kids Can Do
© 2000 Susan L. Lingo

Published by Standard Publishing, Cincinnati, Ohio
A division of Standex International Corporation

Credits
Produced by Susan L. Lingo, Bright Ideas Books™
Cover design by Diana Walters
Illustrated by Marilynn G. Barr

07 06 05 04   5 4 3
0-7847-1154-2
Printed in the United States of America

CONTENTS

GET SET TO SERVE!

What's more fun than having someone surprise you? Surprising someone else! And especially when that surprise is something cool, caring, or clever you do for another person. Jesus spent his entire life as a perfect role model for a servant of God—humble, caring, kind, and compassionate; always putting others before himself through love, forgiveness, and servitude. Paul also recognized that serving enriches our lives and encourages others when he said, "Serve one another in love" (Galatians 5:13). Serving isn't something that only draws us closer to others, it draws us nearer to God himself and the fruit of the Spirit that God desires us to produce and share.

101 Simple Service Projects Kids Can Do encourages kids of all ages to embrace serving as a lifestyle and not just as a "someday, sometime" whim. By putting their faith, love, and sharing into action, kids learn that even the simplest acts of serving touch lives in ways they might never have imagined—and continue to spiral outward in waves of shared compassion and caring! Each service project in this book, no matter how simple, is based on a portion of the Serving Spiral to help kids see that serving has God at its center as it reaches outward to encompass others, including family, friends, the church, the community, and the world. (Look for the Serving Spiral icon in each service project to see whose lives your love will touch!)

Not enough time to serve? Oops, that's not an excuse any longer! *101 Simple Service Projects Kids Can Do* offers five categories of serving so you can choose and use projects to fit any time period or level of involvement. From mini fund-raisers to quick acts of kindness (or "Quaks," as we call 'em!), there's a project—and a purpose—for everyone!

Lead kids joyfully into the Lord's service as you challenge and encourage them to put their love, faith, time, and talents to work for God and others. And remember: we can change the world for Christ—one loving act at a time!

"Serve one another in love." (Galatians 5:13)

Simply Serving

"SERVE ONE ANOTHER IN
LOVE.... 'LOVE YOUR
NEIGHBOR AS YOURSELF.'"

Galatians 5:13,14

SIMPLY SERVING

Welcome to the simplest, surest, sweetest ways to bring God's love to others and to the kids in your classroom! These snappy service projects are easy-to-do, and most can be accomplished within the space of one classtime or less. With a few simple supplies and a bit of serving background, your kids will be touching lives in no time—and the results will last a lifetime. Use these projects anytime you want your kids to experience firsthand the joys and jubilation of "making a difference" as they learn about what it means to be a servant of the Lord!

SPARKLE SPRAY!

Community/
Church

We shine like new when we love Jesus!
Service Scripture: 2 Corinthians 5:17

GET READY...

This summertime service project is guaranteed to put smiles on faces and sparkles on windshields! You'll need a Bible, newspapers, paper towels, and a spray bottle of Special Sparkle window cleaner for every three children. To make Special Sparkle cleaner, mix one part white vinegar to three parts water, then pour into empty spray bottles. You'll also need photocopies of the Care Card poem from the top of page 119.

Special Note: If you can organize this project on a Saturday, consider cleaning police cars or other city vehicles. Be sure to ask for permission. Otherwise, simply arrange to clean your congregation's windshields on a sunny Sunday morning!

GET SET...

Hold up the spray cleaner and a paper towel. Invite a child to clean a dusty table, floorboard, or window. Show kids the dirty paper towel, then ask:

⚘ **How can dirty, dusty things such as windows keep us from seeing clearly?**

⚘ **How are dusty windows like our lives before knowing Jesus?**

Explain that our lives are much like dusty or dirty windows that may block our view with undesirable things such as envy, hate, bad words, lies, and more. Tell kids we need a special cleaner to help us sparkle and shine like new! Then invite a child to read aloud 2 Corinthians 5:17 and 1 John 1:9. Ask:

⚘ **In what ways are Jesus' love and forgiveness like special cleaners for our hearts and lives?**

⚘ **How can being a new creation in Jesus help us live better? serve others? love God more?**

Remind kids that when we know, love, and follow Jesus and when we accept his forgiveness for our sins, we'll be new creations—sparkly and fresh! Tell kids that your special service project today is to remind others how great it is to have sparkly new lives in Jesus!

GO SERVE!

Form groups of three or four and distribute the following to each group: several paper towels, newspapers, several copies of the Sparkle Poem, and a spray bottle of cleaner. Explain that you'll be cleaning windshields, headlights, and car mirrors, then leaving a special poem to read. Have kids take turns being Sprayers, Towelers, and Shiners. Sprayers will spritz on the cleaner. Towelers will wipe the areas with paper towels, and Shiners can make final swoops with newspaper wads to remove any streaks. Remind kids to leave a Sparkle Poem under the windshield wiper of each car they clean.

As kids serve, encourage them to chat about ways Jesus helps us see things more clearly, for example, the truth about God and ourselves.

When you're done, clean up the area and toss out used paper towels and newspapers. End with a group prayer thanking God for the chance to serve others and remind them about Jesus' love and forgiveness.

Your windows are clean, and oh what a view; Jesus' love and forgiveness makes us sparkle like new!

Therefore, if anyone is in Christ, he is a new creation; the old has gone, the new has come! (2 Corinthians 5:17)

TRINITY BRACELET

Church

The Trinity helps us serve others.

Service Scripture: Psalm 118:7; John 14:16, 17

GET READY...

Collect several boxes of small paper clips and tiny seed-beads in a variety of colors. Place the seed-beads and paper clips in muffin tins so several kids can choose colors at the same time and keep the beads from spilling. Children will use paper clips and beads to make two bracelets each—one to wear and one to share! You'll also need a Bible.

GET SET...

Read aloud Psalm 118:7a and John 14:16, 17. Ask kids to explain how God, Jesus, and the Holy Spirit each help us to serve other people. Then ask:

- ✆ **How does God's power help us to serve him?**
- ✆ **In what ways do Jesus' love and forgiveness help us serve?**
- ✆ **How does the power of the Holy Spirit enable us to help others?**

Remind kids that God sent Jesus to love us and to teach us about serving others. Then tell them that Jesus sent the Holy Spirit to empower and enable us to do his work of loving and serving others. Point out that when we use the power of the Trinity, we're able to serve other people in life-changing ways!

Serve one another in love ... 'Love your neighbor as yourself.'

Have kids thread three white beads on one paper clip to represent God's power, then thread three yellow beads on another paper clip to symbolize Christ's love and forgiveness. Finally, have kids thread three red beads on a paper clip to represent the fiery power of the Holy Spirit, which enables us to serve others and God. Show kids how to link the three paper clips together to represent the Trinity.

GO SERVE!

Tell kids the rest of their bracelets will be made up of paper clips with other colors of beads to stand for all the ways there are to serve people, such as through our time, talents, and gifts. Have kids work to thread beads and link paper clips until they've made bracelets large enough to slip over their hands. As kids thread colored beads on the paper clips, encourage them to name ways of serving others and God, such as by saying encouraging words, by doing someone's chores, or by donating clothing or food to a local shelter.

When everyone is wearing a bracelet, have kids make one more to share with someone in another class as a reminder of how the Trinity empowers us to serve others and God in many, colorful ways!

GIVE-N-GET!

Community

We can share God's Word.

Service Scripture: Colossians 3:16

GET READY...

You'll need Bibles, staplers, white paper, scissors, markers, and old wallpaper books (available at home center or decorating stores for free). Cut the sheets of white paper in half lengthwise. Be sure you have a "healthy stack" of paper!

GET SET...

Invite kids to form pairs, and be sure each pair has a Bible. Have kids find a favorite verse in the Bible to read aloud together to the whole group. (If kids have trouble finding verses, encourage them to look in the book of Psalms.) After partners read their verses aloud, ask:

- **In what ways does God's Word teach us about living? about being close to God? about loving and serving others?**
- **Why is God's Word a wonderful gift to share with others?**
- **How is sharing God's Word a good way to serve God? to serve others?**

Read aloud Colossians 3:16. Remind kids that God gives us his Word to live by, to obey, and to teach us how to live with other people in peace, love, and joy. Explain that today's service project involves collecting books for a local children's home. To collect these books, you'll give others parts of the best book ever—the Bible! This way, you'll be serving children by donating books, serving book donors by sharing God's Word, and serving God by spreading his Word!

GO SERVE!

Let kids work in pairs as they make and assemble several books. Have kids stack two half-sheets of paper and fold them in half. Cut book covers from wallpaper pages and staple them with the blank pages into small books. Instruct kids to write Bible verses and draw accompanying pictures on the first three pages. Leave the fourth page blank for people to add their own favorite verses. Title this page "Add Your Own Verse!" Encourage children to use Galatians 5:13 and Colossians 3:16 as verses to copy and illustrate.

As kids work, challenge them to memorize the verses they're adding to their books. Be sure each person makes two or three books to exchange for book donations. Encourage kids to approach friends, neighbors, and family members and to ask them to give a book and get a book in return. Collect the donated books in a colorful box and present them to a children's home or children's hospital.

SURVIVAL KIT

Blessings keep us afloat!

Service Scripture: Deuteronomy 28:2; Psalm 21:6

GET READY...

This simple—yet simply super—service project requires collecting several items for each survival kit. For each kit you'll need a white clasp-style envelope, a toothpick, a rubber band, a pencil, an eraser, a piece of gum, a chocolate candy kiss, a mint, and a copy of the Survival Kit List on page 12. You'll also need markers and a Bible.

GET SET...

Gather kids and ask them to describe what a survival kit is and what value it has. Suggestions might include "a survival kit helps when you have troubles," "it helps in an emergency," and "it can save your life." Then ask:

- **In what ways is the Lord like a survival kit?**
- **How can Jesus' love help us in ways similar to a survival kit?**
- **How can our love help others during their times of trouble?**

Remind kids that sometimes we feel very sad or down and that a reminder of God's love is like a heavenly survival kit. Explain that remembering how many blessings God sends our way often helps us when we're going through troubles. Read aloud Deuteronomy 28:2; Psalm 21:6; and Colossians 3:12-14. Then explain that you'll be making cool survival kits for friends or family members to help them remember God's blessings during tough times.

GO SERVE!

Have kids decorate the large envelopes with red crosses and write the words to Galatians 5:13 across the lower portions of the envelopes.

Write "Survival Kit" across the tops. Then let each child fill a kit with one of each item: a toothpick, a rubber band, a pencil, an eraser, a piece of gum, a mint, a chocolate candy kiss, and a copy of the Survival Kit List that explains the significance of each item. As kids work, have them discuss times they could have used a special reminder of God's love and his Word to help them. Then read through the Survival Kit List and ask kids how each item might have helped them during those times.

When the survival kits are complete, encourage kids to present them to family members or special friends who could use some encouragement and a reminder of God's presence in their lives.

Survival Kit List

Read these reminders to stay afloat when life gets you down.

- **toothpick:** This small piece of wood reminds us of the large gift of love Jesus gave us on the cross.
- **rubber band:** When situations stretch you, God helps you remain flexible.
- **pencil:** Smile! God has already written your name in his book of life!
- **eraser:** God "erases" our sins and mistakes when we ask for his forgiveness.
- **gum:** God's love and presence sticks with us through thick and thin.
- **mint:** Remember the sweetness and comfort that is found in God's Word.
- **chocolate candy kiss:** God sent us the kiss of love and life through Jesus.

T.E.a.M. WÖRK!

Together we accomplish great things for God.

Service Scripture: Acts 4:32; 1 Corinthians 3:9

GET READY...

Collect colorful pony beads, fine-tipped permanent markers, and key chains or satin cord. (If you choose to use satin cord, you'll also need several pairs of scissors.) You'll need enough materials for each child to make two or three key chains. You'll also need a Bible.

GET SET...

Invite kids to help separate the beads into piles, one pile for each color. (If you are using satin cords, ask kids to cut them into 6-inch lengths.) Praise kids for working well together and for helping one another through teamwork. Then ask:

- **In what ways is teamwork better than working alone? Which allows us to accomplish more and why?**
- **How are church members working together a good example of teamwork for God? for others?**

Read aloud Acts 4:32 and 1 Corinthians 3:9, then tell kids that the letters T-E-A-M stand for Together Everyone Accomplishes More! Remind kids that this is true for everyone working together in church, too. Then tell kids they'll make neat key chains to give to adults to remind them that together everyone accomplishes more—in and out of church!

Go SERVE!

Have kids help each other prepare the key chains. You'll need four pony beads for each chain. Use the fine-tipped markers to write the letter T on one bead, E on another, A on the third bead, and M on the fourth. When the ink is dry, string the beads on a key chain or piece of satin cord so they spell the word TEAM. Tie the ends of the satin cord.

Serve one another in love ... 'love your neighbor as yourself.'

Have each child make several key chains so you have enough to share with the adult Sunday school classes. Share a prayer asking God's help in showing your church how to work together to accomplish God's will and reach others with the message about Jesus' love.

PACKED WiTH LOVE

Community

God uses us to provide for others.

Service Scripture: Galatians 5:13; Romans 12:13

GET READY...

Prior to this project, hold a food drive to collect plenty of the following items: small bags of chips, packaged cookies or peanuts, apples and bananas, individual juice boxes or pouches, and individual containers of prepared foods such as tuna and crackers or cans of beans and franks. You'll also need plastic tableware, napkins, index cards, markers, large self-sealing plastic bags, and a Bible.

GET SET...

After the food is collected, place it in the center of a table or on the floor. Gather kids around the food offerings and ask:

- **How is God's provision for us packed with his love?**
- **Why is it important to help others? to pack our help with love?**
- **How does this bring us closer to God? to others?**

Tell kids that when God provides for us, he packs his provision with love and caring. Read aloud Galatians 5:13 and Romans 12:13. Then remind kids that when we serve others and help provide for their needs, we can pack a lot of love into our serving! Explain that you'll be packing special lunches to provide for others in the community.

Serve one another in love ... 'Love your neighbor as yourself.'

GO SERVE!

Have kids separate the foods into drinks, fruit, chips, prepared foods, and dessert. Then let kids work in assembly-line style to pack lunches that include one of each item as well as napkins and tableware. Let some of the kids use markers and index cards to make cheery cards. Write "Packed with love! Galatians 5:13" on the cards. Be sure to place a card in each lunch bag. Deliver the lunches to a local food pantry or to Meals on Wheels. (You may want to get prior permission for your special donations.)

HAVE A BALL!

Community/ Friends

Jesus is our best friend.

Service Scripture: John 15:15

GET READY...

This simple service project will bring smiles to young children's faces and let them know that their best friend is Jesus! You'll need several bouncy, vinyl balls. (Choose solid colors!) You'll also need colorful permanent markers and a Bible.

GET SET...

Gather kids in a circle and roll a ball back and forth as children tell their names. Point out how we're all friends who have a common best friend—Jesus! Read aloud John 15:15b, then ask:

⊚ **What does it mean that Jesus calls us his friends?**

⚙ **What makes a good friend?**

⚙ **In what ways is Jesus our best friend?**

Remind kids that Jesus served all people and not just his friends. Point out that we can also serve people we may not even know because they may become our friends! Tell kids you'll serve young children, whom Jesus especially calls his friends, by making a fun reminder of Jesus' friendship.

GO SERVE!

Have kids form as many small groups as you have bouncy balls. Invite each group to decorate the playground ball using the brightly colored permanent markers, then write the words "Jesus calls you his friend" around the center of each ball. Then let each child in the group draw a small picture of himself on the ball and sign his name. As kids work, encourage them to tell how we can be friendly to people we may not even know.

After the bouncy balls are finished, play a quick game of Call-Ball. Ask kids to form a large circle, then have someone toss a ball in the air and call out a child's name. The person called rushes forward to catch the ball.

End by offering a prayer for the young children who will receive your special gifts, asking God that they will know Jesus as their best friend! Donate the bouncy balls to a local day-care center or Head Start program.

KINDNESS COUNTS

A five-year-old, hearing-impaired boy in Colorado proved his heart was much bigger and warmer than any fuzzy blanket! This young boy wanted to help families left homeless after a fire in an area motel. With the help of his parents, he collected cash contributions and was able to buy sixty fuzzy blankets for the families. Local firefighters delivered the gifts and warm love brought through the blankets. You're never too young to serve!

GREAT GREETINGS

We can invite others to church.

Service Scripture: 1 Thessalonians 3:2; 1 Peter 5:2

GET READY...

For this clever service project, you'll need to gather construction paper, index cards, glue sticks, markers, and scissors. You'll also need a Bible, a camera, and plenty of film (instant cameras are ideal).

GET SET...

Have kids each tell three other children their favorite thing about your church. It may be the friendly people, perhaps it's the fun learning and Bible games, or maybe kids enjoy the church picnics and parties. Remind kids that the more people who belong to your church, the more fun and teamwork there is—and the more people there are to praise the Lord! Explain that pastors and others at the church go into the community to visit people and invite them to your church, just as Paul did in the New Testament. Read aloud 1 Peter 5:2 and 1 Thessalonians 3:2. Then ask:

- **Why is it important to welcome others to our church?**
- **In what ways can we be welcoming when others visit our church?**

Remind kids that Jesus wants everyone to know, love, and follow him and that we can serve by helping other people feel welcome at church. Explain that you'll be making welcome cards for your church leaders to present to prospective church members and others who may visit your church.

GO SERVE!

Let kids take photos of themselves, the church, any colorful displays that may be up, and other interesting aspects of your church or church

Serve one another in love ... 'Love your neighbor as yourself.'

family. As photos are being taken, have other kids prepare construction-paper cards with the words "Welcome" or "Come Join Us!" on the covers. Invite kids to write on index cards their names and ages and one thing they especially enjoy about your church. Glue the index cards to one side of the insides of the welcome cards. When the photos are finished (either instantly or after being developed), glue them to the opposite sides of the index cards. End by offering a prayer for new people who may be attending or preparing to attend your church.

Present your special greeting cards to the pastor or other church leader to give to families and prospective church members.

BEAUTIFUL FEET!

Community/ World

It's important to tell others about Jesus.

Service Scripture: Isaiah 52:7

GET READY...

This simple back-to-school service idea can double as a community and a world missions project—it's up to you and your kids! To "get in step" with this project, you'll need pairs of new socks, large manila envelopes, shoelaces, glue sticks, colorful markers, glitter-glue pens, and photocopies of Isaiah 52:7 or Romans 10:15. Make the copies on bright neon paper, then cut the verses apart to make colorful verse cards.

Either purchase new socks in bulk from a discount store, ask for donations from the congregation, or have kids each bring in one or two new pairs of socks to share with someone in the community. Be sure you have a selection of socks for boys and girls in a variety of sizes and styles.

GET SET...

Place the pairs of socks, shoelaces, envelopes, verse cards, and craft items in separate piles in the center of the room. Gather kids around the piles and have them tell about the best part of back-to-school time. Suggestions might include gathering school supplies, meeting new friends, and buying new clothes and shoes. Remind kids that not everyone starting a new school year has money to purchase new clothes, including socks or shoes. Read aloud Isaiah 52:7 or Romans 10:15, then ask:

- **How can this verse remind us of the importance of helping others?**
- **In what ways is bringing the good news about Jesus a way to serve someone?**

Explain that this back-to-school service project will bring the good news about Jesus' love to others as it brings new socks for happy feet!

GO SERVE!

Have each child collect a pair of socks, shoelaces, a verse card, and a manila envelope. Invite kids to serve one another by tracing each other's feet on the backs of the manila envelopes, then have them write the sock sizes and the words "boy's" or "girl's" inside the foot outlines. Glue the verse cards to the outsides of the envelopes. Decorate the envelopes using markers and glitter glue. Thread pairs of shoelaces through the clasp holes of the envelopes. Place a pair of socks inside each envelope and seal the envelope securely.

As kids work, encourage them to say words of thanks for the wonderful items they have for their own back-to-school supplies. When all of the packages are finished, place them in the center of the floor and share a prayer asking God to carry your happy donations to children who really need them—and need to hear the good news about Jesus! Give your donations to a family shlter, children's home, or hospital.

LEND A HAND!

Church

Let's encourage one another!

Service Scripture: Ephesians 4:32; Philippians 1:4-6

Serve one another in love … 'Love your neighbor as yourself.'

GET READY...

This whimsical service project is a fun way for kids to reach everyone in the church to remind them that encouraging others and lending their helping hands are wonderful ways to serve others with love! Set up tables where everyone can make these cool "clappers" and station your kids at the tables after class to offer their service and help. You'll need plenty of scissors, glitter glue, colored poster board, markers, wire cutters, 19-gauge wire, clear packing tape, and a Bible.

GET SET...

Make a springy hand according to the directions below, then give everyone loving pats and encouraging high fives as they arrive. Ask:

- **When was a time you encouraged someone with a simple act such as a handshake, pat, hug, or high five?**
- **How can simple acts of serving help others as much as large projects?**
- **Who can you encourage today with a pat, a handshake, and a hug?**

Read aloud Ephesians 4:32 and Philippians 1:4-6. Remind kids that when we serve in even the smallest of ways, we're serving and loving God, too. Give each child another loving pat, hug, or high five, then tell kids that lending a real hand to help is what serving others is all about! Explain that today you'll be making (and helping others make) cool clapper-hands to give pats, hugs, handshakes, and fun reminders about lending our helping hands in God's service!

GO SERVE!

Have kids each trace one of their hands on poster board and cut the paper hand out. Use markers and glitter glue to decorate the paper hands, then tape the base of the hands to 3-foot lengths of 19-gauge wire with clear packing tape.

When the hands are done, invite kids to give someone a pat, someone else a hug, and a third person a handshake with their happy hands. Then have kids serve the church congregation by helping everyone make their own happy serving hands after church. Encourage kids to challenge the people they help to lend their hands in some way to serve others this week.

KINDNESS COUNTS

What started as a babysitting club for a small group of sixth-grade girls in the south turned into a wonderful service project to help young, disadvantaged moms. The girls would see many young mothers struggle to provide diapers, formula, and warm blankets for their babies. In response, the girls collected bags of baby items, including diapers, bibs, formula, and toys to present to young moms at local shelters and in the community. Oh baby—what a wonderful way to serve!

CUP OF COCO-JOE  Community

Serving makes us feel good.

Service Scripture: Romans 12:11

GET READY...

Collect the following items and place them on a table: a box of self-sealing plastic sandwich bags, several large containers of instant coffee creamer, a large can of cocoa, a large box of powdered sugar, curling ribbon, scissors, tape, measuring cups, a mixing bowl, plastic spoons, and a Bible. You'll also need to photocopy the Care Card from the bottom of page 119 on bright paper.

GET SET...

Invite kids to tell about how it feels when someone helps them or does something kind for them. After several kids share, read aloud Romans 12:11, then ask:

- ✺ **In what does serving make us feel warm and good inside?**
- ✺ **Why is it important to do kind things for people outside of our families?**
- ✺ **How does this draw us closer to God? to others?**

Tell kids that many people don't have good, warm homes to live in but must visit shelters to get warm, especially in cold weather. Explain that we can get warm in different ways. We can cover up with a blanket, go indoors when it's cold, or drink hot chocolate to warm us. We can also feel warm on the inside when we know someone cares for us! Tell kids you'll be making a special treat for homeless people in the area to warm them with hot cocoa—and with God's love and our caring!

GO SERVE!

In the mixing bowl, mix 4 cups of instant creamer, 2 cups of cocoa, and 2 cups of powdered sugar. Spoon four spoonfuls of Coco-Joe mix into each self-sealing bag, then place a plastic spoon in each bag and seal the bag tightly. Tape curling ribbon to the top of each bag and add a Care Card. Each bag will make two cups of Coco-Joe hot chocolate or can be used as a special creamer in four cups of coffee!

GOD HAS LOVED YOU FROM THE START— HERE'S SOMETHING ELSE TO WARM YOUR HEART!

Mix 2 spoonfuls in a cup of hot water or 1 spoonful in hot coffee.

"Be devoted to one another in brotherly love. Honor one another above yourselves." Romans 12:10

STRESS-STUFFIES

6 Family

We need lots of patience and love!

Service Scripture: Romans 5:3, 4; 1 Thessalonians 5:14

GET READY...

This neat family service idea will squeeze the stress out of tense tiffs! For each Stress-Stuffy, you'll need an uninflated balloon (helium quality) and ⅓ cup of flour. You'll also need scissors, funnels, permanent markers, and a Bible. Each child will make two Stress-Stuffies.

GET SET...

Invite kids to think about a time family members might have disagreed, argued, or been in a tense situation. Assure kids that when people live so closely together as in families, there are bound to be a few rough spots and waves even when we love each other! Ask:

- **What things can make our families tense, tired, or stressed?** (Suggestions might include jobs, school, fatigue, money worries, and even age differences.)
- **How can we handle stressful situations in loving ways?**

Explain that ways to handle family problems or disagreements might include listening and discussing problems, trying to see things from the other person's point of view, and taking a "breather" before responding. Point out that almost all problems can be overcome through love and patience.

Read aloud Romans 5:3, 4 and 1 Thessalonians 5:14. Then explain that you'll be making family Stress-Stuffies to give family members a "breather" so they can respond to one another in healthy, loving ways.

GO SERVE!

Show kids how to stretch their balloons by blowing them up, then letting the air out of them. Place a funnel at the opening of the balloon

Serve one another in love ... 'Love your neighbor as yourself.'

and pour in ⅓ cup flour. Knot the balloons at the top of the flour and cut off any extra balloon material. Have kids use markers to draw comical faces on the Stress-Stuffies. As kids work, explain that the Stress-Stuffies are to be squeezed when someone is feeling upset, frustrated, angry, or stressed out. Explain that, as the Stuffies are squeezed, there's time to think about healthy ways of responding to feelings, such as through listening, calmly talking things out, or praying for God's guidance and patience.

When the Stress-Stuffies are complete, have kids sit in a circle and squeeze the stuffed balloons as you share a prayer asking for God's love and patience to be upon families so they respond to one another in calm, loving ways. Challenge kids to explain to their families how the stuffies are used and to try them out this week.

SWEET THANKS

Church

We can thank church helpers.
Service Scripture: 2 Timothy 1:3

GET READY...

Kids will enjoy this clever thank-you for church leaders, workers, and other volunteers. For each edible thank-you, you'll need a roll (or mini roll) of Life Savers brand candies and a 20-inch shoelace. You'll also need tape, sharpened pencils or knitting needles, a Bible, and copies of the Care Card from the top of page 120.

GET SET...

Invite four or five kids to stand up front, side by side in a row. Hand a child on one end of the row a Bible, then explain that she is to get the

Bible to the other end of the line without moving from her place. (In other words, kids will pass the Bible down to the opposite end of the row.) Then instruct the child holding the Bible to open to 2 Timothy 1:3 and to whisper it to the person next to her to "pass" it down the line to the child at the opposite end of the row. Ask the group:

- ☙ **In what ways did each person play an active role in passing both the Bible and verse?**
- ☙ **How is this like the way many people helping at church accomplish things? draw others to God and his Word?**

Explain that there are many leaders, volunteers, and helpers at church who play active roles in serving God and spreading his Word and love to others. Point out that some leaders and helpers have more visibly active roles, just like the kids at both ends of the passing row. But tell kids that many people at church help in ways we may not notice as easily and that we want to be sure everyone's contributions and help are appreciated!

Explain that today you'll demonstrate your appreciation of the many times church volunteers go out of their way to help. Point out that during parties, worship services, special programs, and other busy times, these leaders and helpers are like "lifesavers" for the church! Tell kids you'll be making sweet thank-yous for the many times leaders and helpers are lifesavers.

THANKS!

THANKS!

THANKS!

THANKS!

Thanks for being a real lifesaver
Who loves and serves our real life Savior!
Philippians 1:3, 4

Go Serve!

Have kids work in pairs if they'd like. For each edible thank-you, you'll need to poke a hole in each end of the aluminum Life Savers wrapper. Use a sharp pencil or knitting needle and be sure to help young kids so they do not poke themselves. Thread a shoelace through the center of the roll of Life Savers, then tie the ends to make a necklace. Tape a Care Card to each roll of candy. Be sure to make plenty of edible thank-yous to hand out to all who lead, volunteer, and are general "lifesavers" in your church!

CHORE-GRABBERS

Family

We can serve cheerfully and willingly!

Service Scripture: Ephesians 6:7; 1 Peter 5:2

GET READY...

Encourage kids to make these cool Chore-Grabbers and grab the chore of washing dishes or other cleaning away from Mom or Dad! You'll need rubber bands, scissors, several packages of disposable towelettes, and several yards of colorful mesh netting. Cut the netting into 12-inch squares. Each child will need two cloth wipes, four squares of netting, and two rubber bands. Make a Chore-Grabber ahead of time to show to kids. Be sure to keep a Bible handy.

GET SET...

Ask kids to name some of the many things Jesus did for us. Suggestions might include healing, praying, teaching, loving, encouraging, leading, forgiving, and dying for our sins. Read aloud Ephesians 6:7 and 1 Peter 5:2, then ask:

- **Why do you think Jesus did so many things for us?**
- **Do you think Jesus looked on these actions as chores or as acts of love? Explain.**
- **How is this like the way we can approach "chores" for our families and the people we love?**

Remind kids that Jesus did many things for us because he loves us so greatly. Point out that our parents and other loving adults do many things for us because they love us, too. Explain that kids can demonstrate their own love by cheerfully helping and serving and that sometimes it's fun to serve others by doing their chores! Tell kids you'll make neat Chore-Grabbers to demonstrate your love and caring by grabbing away someone else's chores this week.

GO SERVE!

For each Chore-Grabber, cut two cloth wipes in half. Place the cloths in a pile to the left and four 12-inch squares of netting in a pile to the right, slightly overlapping the ends of the cloth as in the illustration. Join the cloth and netting by securely wrapping a rubber band around the center. Next, fold the far ends of the cloth and netting to the center and wrap another rubber band to secure the ends in the middle of the grabber. You should have a butterfly-shaped Chore-Grabber with one cloth end and one netting end! Now you're ready for dusting, polishing, scrubbing, scouring—and showering others with love!

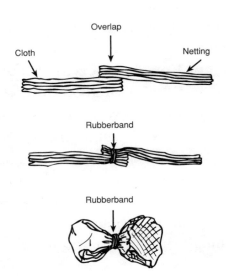

FILL 'ER UP!

Community

Serving fills us with love!

Service Scripture: Romans 12:10

GET READY...

Before this simply wonderful service project, contact several Christian stores that sell books and gift items and use paper bags to sack them. Suggestions might include Christian bookstores, grocers, gift shops, and thrift stores. Ask the managers if your kids can decorate colorful sacks that remind others to help and serve one another. Either use the sacks they have on hand or collect paper lunch sacks or grocery bags to decorate. You'll need colorful markers, glitter glue, crayons, glue sticks, scissors, and bright copies of the Care Card rhyme from the bottom of page 120. Place the craft supplies and a Bible in a large paper bag.

GET SET...

Place the bag containing the craft items and Bible in front of the kids and tell them that the bag is filled with love and other good things, then invite them to guess what might be inside. After the guesses, ask:

⚙ **How does serving fill us with good things like this bag is filled with good things?**

⚙ **In what ways does helping others fill them with love and good feelings? fill God's heart with love?**

Read aloud Romans 12:10 and the serving rhyme kids will place on the paper sacks later. Remind kids that when we serve others, we're serving God, too. Tell kids that when we take the time to help others, even in the simplest of ways, we fill our hearts and lives with good things such as love, caring, and generosity.

Show kids the contents of the bag, then explain that these good things will be used to make colorful sacks to remind others how we fill ourselves and others with love when we serve! Point out that the items in the sack have the potential to be helpful but only when they're taken out and used. Explain that lovingkindness is much the same way—it's inside us but must be taken out and put to use to help others!

GO SERVE!

Let kids work in small groups to decorate the paper sacks. Suggest designs that are cheerful and promote messages of peace and love, such as heart shapes, doves, flowers, and stars. Be sure to glue a copy of the Care Card rhyme to each sack. As kids work, tell them which stores will give out the super serving sacks, then end by offering a prayer for those stores and the customers who will receive your colorful sacks full of love!

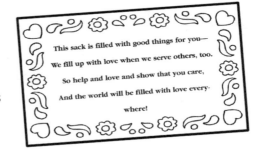

This sack is filled with good things for you—
We fill up with love when we serve others, too.
So help and love and show that you care,
And the world will be filled with love everywhere!

SHINE ON

Family

We can carry God's love to new places.

Service Scripture: Numbers 6:24-26

GET READY...

This unique project will bring a glow to the hearts of anyone moving in or out of your church family. You'll need toothpicks, a nonstick electric skillet, a chunky pillar candle for each child, and several bags of colorful wax chips (available at most craft stores). You'll also need a Bible, markers, index cards, and plastic wrap or tissue paper.

GET SET...

Preheat the electric skillet on medium heat. Invite kids to tell about times they may have moved to a new house or town or about new people in their neighborhoods. Ask:

- **In what ways can moving be hard or even scary? In other words, how can moving sometimes feel like being in a dark, lonely, and unfamiliar place?**
- **How can God's love help during a move? How can we help encourage others who are new or moving?**

Read aloud Numbers 6:24-26 and point out how these verses give a blessing to remind us that God is always with us no matter where we may be. Remind kids that moving can be a difficult time for many people and that having a warm reminder of God's love and our own love can lighten hearts and brighten new homes. Explain that you'll be making beautiful housewarming candles to warm up and light the lives of people "on the move" in or out of your church family.

GO SERVE!

Show kids how to poke the toothpicks into the surface of wax chips. Hold the chips on the surface of the electric skillet for a moment, then quickly stick the chip to a pillar candle. The wax from the chip and the candle will melt together and hold the wax chips in place like colorful mosaics! Decorate the candles, then let kids each write a short, encouraging note on index cards. Have them write "The Lord bless you and keep you" (the priestly blessing from Numbers 6:24) on the index cards. Then wrap each candle and a card in plastic wrap or tissue paper.

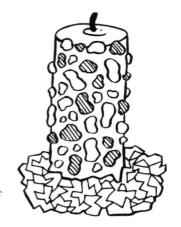

Offer a prayer for people moving in and out of your church, then keep the candles in the church office to hand out as needed.

STAR OF THE BIBLE!

Friends

God is the star of the Bible!

Service Scripture: 2 Timothy 3:16

GET READY...

Kids will love this crafty project as they help introduce their friends to the Bible, God's Word! You'll need a Bible, colorful star-shaped confetti (either purchase the confetti or use glittery star stickers), a roll of clear packing tape, scissors, a jar of glitter, a hole punch, and bright yarn. If you want to make this a really meaningful project, purchase small copies of the Bible or the New Testament to present along with your starry bookmarks.

GET SET...

Invite kids to tell about their favorite books and why they like them so much. Encourage kids to tell if the books have lessons in them or teach about great people. Tell kids you know of a book that has sold more copies than any other book in history, that teaches about life, and that stars the most powerful being in the universe! Ask kids to identify the book you're talking about (the Bible), then ask:

- **Why is the Bible the most important book in the world?**
- **How is God the star of the Bible? Are there other stars? Who are they?**
- **Why do you think the Bible is the best-seller of all time?**

Read aloud 2 Timothy 3:16. Then hold up the Bible and remind kids that the Bible is inspired by God and contains all his truths and teaching for every area of our lives. Explain that some people aren't familiar with God's gift of the Bible, so God wants us to help others learn about the Bible and its stars, including God, Jesus, the Holy Spirit, and many great people such as Moses, David, Ruth, and Mary. Tell kids that you'll make cool, glittering, star-studded bookmarks to remind others that the star of the Bible—God—wants us to learn and love his Word!

GO SERVE!

For each bookmark, cut a 16-inch length of clear packing tape and place it on a table with the sticky side facing up. Sprinkle stars and glitter on half of the sticky tape. Then carefully fold the tape in half and stick the two sides together so the stars and glitter stay sandwiched between the tape. If the edges of the tape don't quite meet, you can trim them with scissors. (For classes of young children, you may wish to use clear self-adhesive paper instead of packing tape, since the paper is easier to work with.) The folded end of the tape is the top of the bookmark. Use scissors to round the bottom end of the bookmark, then punch a hole near the top. Tie several 6-inch lengths of yarn through the hole to make pretty tassels.

Offer a prayer asking God to lead others to his Word and to help them read the Bible every day to learn about God and his love! Present the bookmarks (and small Bibles or New Testaments if you chose to purchase them) to friends who will enjoy learning about God and his Word!

FUNNIES FUN

We can seek Jesus anywhere!

Service Scripture: Ecclesiastes 4:9, 10

GET READY...

This get-acquainted service project is perfect for back-to-school time or anytime you want your kids to host a fun 'n friendly event for peers. You'll need a Bible, plenty of colorful Sunday newspaper comics, poster board, markers, glue sticks, scissors, and balloons. For the actual get-together, you'll need graham crackers, colorful tube icing, plastic knives, paper or plastic tableware and cups, and chilled apple juice.

GET SET...

Gather kids and invite them to tell about times they made new friends. Encourage them to share what it was like to meet someone new or how it felt to be someone in a new church, school, or neighborhood. Then ask:

- 🌀 **How is finding a new friend like discovering Jesus in our lives?**
- 🌀 **Where can new friends be found? Where can we find our best friend, Jesus?**
- 🌀 **In what ways does Jesus' loving friendship help us? How can we help others through our own friendliness?**

Point out that just as we seek and find Jesus in all places and in all parts of our lives, we can seek new friends in all places. Read aloud Ecclesiastes 4:9, 10, then ask kids why it's important to be friendly and welcoming to others. Tell kids that this service project is almost like a party to meet new friends at church. Explain that this week, you'll make cool posters to invite kids to your fun 'n friendly get-together and that next week you'll host your exciting event.

Serve one another in love ... 'Love your neighbor as yourself.'

GO SERVE!

Set out the craft items and challenge kids to make colorful posters using cutouts of their "friends" from the funny papers. Title the posters, "Come Join the Fun and Meet New Friends!" To describe your get-together, add phrases such as *fun friends, neat treats,* and *great games.* Decorate the posters with inflated balloons.

Hang the posters around the church or, if you plan on inviting just one other class, present your colorful invitations by hanging them on the walls and shaking class members' hands as you give them personal invitations and balloons.

At your event next week, let kids decorate graham crackers with the faces of their favorite cartoon characters and challenge guests to guess the identities of your cartoon friends. Play several simple games, then form a circle and share a prayer asking Jesus to help each of you become closer and open to making new friends. Then encourage everyone to enjoy the graham crackers and apple juice as they establish and deepen friendships.

KINDNESS COUNTS

A two-year-old girl from Boston recently lost her daddy to a deadly lightning strike. The lightning bolt also burned the little girl. Doctors had trouble bandaging her leg until a mysterious package showed up for the tot. A tiny bean-bag kitty was given to the little girl and has since become her "best friend." When the bandages were changed on her leg, the doctors even bandaged the kitty's leg! A secret act of kindness put a big smile on a little face—and a hug in her heart!

LÖÖK TO SERVE

There are many needs to serve.

Service Scripture: 1 Peter 4:10

GET READY...

For this unusual service project for the elderly, you'll need to collect old, wide neckties. Visit used clothing stores or ask members of the congregation to donate their wide, out-of-style neckties. You'll also need a Bible, scissors, tacky craft glue, and self-adhesive, hook-and-loop dots (such as those made by Velcro USA). You may wish to make a glasses holder before class as a sample.

GET SET...

Have kids close their eyes, then ask them to describe what you're wearing, the color of your eyes, and any other things they may have noticed about you. After several tries, have kids open their eyes to see if they're correct. Tell kids to look closely at you for fifteen seconds, then have them close their eyes again and tell you what they've seen. Ask:

- **Why was it easier to notice things the second time you looked?**
- **How is this like how we sometimes overlook ways to serve others or overlook their needs?**

Remind kids that we all have needs and that God knows our every need and want. Read aloud 1 Peter 4:10, then point out that God knows our needs because he knows us! God sees us all the time and knows us in and out. Explain that we can serve others and meet their needs if we take the time to really look around us and use what God has given us to serve others. Tell kids that many elderly people need glasses to see clearly and that the class can serve them by making colorful glasses cases to hold their eyeglasses. Remind kids that we need both our eyes and our hearts to see other people's needs and to serve them!

GO SERVE!

Invite kids to work in pairs. For each glasses holder, cut a 12-inch long section from the wider end of a necktie, measuring from the pointed tip upward. If the tie has a tag inside, remove it. If the seam is unraveling a bit, seal the seam with tacky glue. Then glue where you cut the straight opening of the tie closed. (You may have to hold it closed for a few minutes until the glue dries.) Next, press two sticky-backed Velcro dots to the tie—one on the inside portion of the tip and one on the tie. These will keep the cases closed and the glasses safe inside!

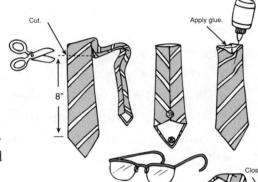

You may wish to make cards to accompany your gifts and explain how the glasses cases are used. End with a prayer for God to help you see the many needs of others and how best to serve them. Present your projects to a senior care center or use them as grandparents' gifts.

SERVING SAFETY

Friends

Jesus is our source of safety.

Service Scripture: Romans 10:13

GET READY...

This clever service project comes with an important message to youth who are driving: Jesus is our source of safety—even in our cars! You'll need a Bible; stiff, colored wire (anodized aluminum or colorful, metal paper clips); alphabet beads; needle-nosed pliers; and round key rings. If you can't find alphabet beads, simply use a fine-tipped permanent

You'll need to cut the colored wire into 5-inch lengths, three for each key ring. You may wish to make a key ring to show kids as a sample.

GET SET... ⊚ ⊚ ⊚

Place the craft items on a table and gather kids around it. Ask kids to tell about people or things that help keep them safe and secure. Then ask:

- ⊚ **In what ways does our faith in Jesus help keep us safe?**
- ⊚ **Why is Jesus our best source of safety?**
- ⊚ **How can other forms of safety or protection fail us? How does it feel to know that Jesus never fails us?**

Read aloud Romans 10:13 and remind kids that Jesus' love, forgiveness, wisdom, and gift of eternal life are our best security and assurance for a "safe landing" in life! Explain that Jesus' love and direction stay with us wherever we are—even traveling in cars! Point out that many teens in your church are driving or learning to drive and may need a special reminder of how Jesus is with them and helping keep them safe. Explain that you'll make cool key-ring reminders for the youth in your church as a super service project.

GO SERVE!

Show kids how to twist, spiral, zigzag, or bend the lengths of colored wire or paper clips into interesting shapes. Tell kids they'll need two bent pieces of wire and one straight piece. On the straight piece of wire, string alphabet beads to spell JESUS. Then bend the end of the wire upward (by the letter S) to keep the beads from slipping off the wire. Bend the top of the wire around a key ring to make a loop so the entire wire can slide around the key ring. Attach the two squiggly pieces of colored wire on either side of the beaded wire by bending them around the key ring. (All three pieces of wire should slide around the key ring freely!)

Serve one another in love ... 'Love your neighbor as yourself.'

36

Offer a prayer for the safety and wisdom of teen drivers and for all drivers. Then present your cool key rings to the members of the youth group. (Be sure to make a few extras for visitors or any absent drivers!)

LIVING WATER!

Jesus is the living water.

Service Scripture: John 4:14

GET READY...

You'll need a Bible, empty 1-gallon plastic milk jugs, colored labeling or electrical tape, scissors, self-sealing plastic sandwich bags, and bulk plant food. If you'd like to make your own plant food, combine old coffee grounds (dried out), crushed egg shells, and bone meal in any concentration. You'll also need a Bible and copies of the Care Card from the top of page 121.

GET SET...

Gather kids and invite them to compare and contrast what plants and humans need to grow healthy. Then ask what we need to also grow happy. Read aloud John 4:14 and ask:

- ☺ **How is Jesus like living water? Why do we need Jesus in our lives?**
- ☺ **In what ways does Jesus help us grow healthy and happy?**

Explain that Jesus brings us life—both now on earth and later in heaven. Point out that all things need water to live and how we need Jesus in our lives to live, love, and be happy. Tell kids that you'll be making colorful watering jugs to present to senior citizens at church and in the community as reminders of Jesus as our living water. Point out that many older adults love gardening and that these water jugs will be great reminders of how things grow and how much we all need Jesus, the living water.

GO SERVE!

Invite kids to work in pairs or trios. For each watering jug, have kids cut pieces of colored tape and stick them in patterns and designs to an empty milk jug. Then attach small bags of plant food to the jugs by using loops of colored tape. As you work, discuss the areas in your lives that Jesus gives growth to, such as your faith, honesty, general character, love, and closeness to God. Tape a Care Card to each jaunty jug.

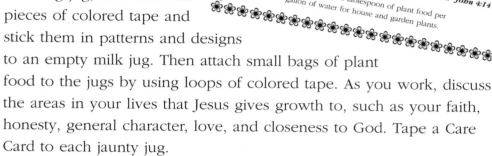

CARE FOR YOUR PLANTS THE WAY YOU 'OUGHTER' AND REMEMBER THAT JESUS IS OUR LIVING WATER!

"Whoever drinks the water I give him will never thirst." John 4:14

Directions: Mix a tablespoon of plant food per gallon of water for house and garden plants.

End by offering a prayer for the seniors who will receive your gifts and ask God that they will seek Jesus and his living water in their lives every day.

SERVING AS JESUS

Church

Serve others in the way Jesus served.

Service Scripture: Matthew 20:28; John 13:14, 15

GET READY...

This unusual project serves church leaders and teachers similar to the way Jesus served—with clever foot washing! You'll need a Bible; Epsom salts; essential oil of lemon, mint, or lavender (available at natural food stores); plastic spoons; self-sealing sandwich bags; a stapler; and copies of the Care Card from the bottom of page 121.

GET SET...

Invite kids to recount ways that Jesus served others. Suggestions might include healing the lepers, raising Lazarus, giving sight to blind Bartimaeus, calming the storm, and forgiving stingy Zacchaeus. Remind kids how Jesus taught us about serving others at the Lord's Supper when he washed the feet of his disciples. Read aloud Matthew 20:28 and John 13:14, 15. Then ask:

- **What did Jesus mean when he said that we must be servants to all?**
- **In what ways did Jesus' foot washing teach us about serving others in even the simplest of ways?**
- **How can we serve others as Jesus served them?**

Explain that there are many ways to serve others and that one way is to recognize, encourage, and thank those who are doing the Lord's work, such as our church leaders and teachers. Tell kids these people run here and there in a tireless effort to teach others about Jesus and bring his love to them. Let kids know you'll honor, serve, and thank these people in a way similar to how Jesus served his disciples—with a unique way to wash their feet!

GO SERVE!

For each foot soak, have kids measure three plastic spoonfuls of Epsom salt and several drops of essential oil into a plastic sandwich bag. Seal the bag and staple a Care Card to the top. If there's time, you might wish to include a decorated thank-you note from kids with each gift bag. As you work, name ways that teachers and church leaders selflessly serve others. Remind kids that serving as Jesus served means being selfless and giving and putting ourselves last and others first!

Offer a prayer of thanks for people who serve God by serving and teaching in church. Then present your gifts to teachers and other church leaders for a relaxing foot soak—and smile!

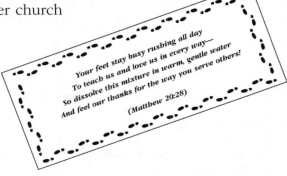

Your feet stay busy rushing all day
To teach us and love us in every way—
So dissolve this mixture in warm, gentle water
And feel our thanks for the way you serve others!

(Matthew 20:28)

Serve one another in love ... 'Love your neighbor as yourself.'

FAMiLY FUN NiGHT

We can encourage families to be close.

Service Scripture: 1 Thessalonians 5:11; Hebrews 10:24, 25

GET READY...

This family and neighborhood outreach is a great way for entire families to serve together! You'll need a Bible, construction paper, markers, graham crackers, canned icing, plastic knives, and small candies to decorate goodies.

GET SET...

Invite kids to tell about fun activities or traditions they share with their families. Suggestions could include movie nights, story time, family devotions, and special vacations with Grandma and Grandpa. Read aloud Hebrews 10:24, 25 and 1 Thessalonians 5:1. Then ask:

- **Why is it important for families to draw close to God? to each other?**
- **How does encouraging family closeness encourage closeness to God?**

Explain that many families enjoy Family Fun Nights, when they invite neighbors or friends to share in an evening of fun away from telephones, television, and troubles! Tell kids that during these nights, families share games, crafts, good food, and lots of fun. Explain that today you'll plan out a simple Family Fun Night kids and their families can host at home.

GO SERVE!

Turn children loose making colorful invitations to their Family Fun Night festivities. List words such as *food, fun,* and *games* on the invitations. (Don't list times yet, since kids must check with families for their permission first!) Stress that each family can share their own together-time or invite another family to join in the fun! Challenge kids to brainstorm simple games to play, including Simon Says, Hide-and-Seek, Tiddlywinks, Pick-Up Sticks, and building card houses. Then invite kids to name several other activities to share, such as reading favorite stories, acting out charades of biblical characters, or making colorful paper airplanes to race and fly.

Let kids decorate several graham-cracker treats with icing and small candies to inspire them to make fun foods to share—or let their guests make their own on the special family night.

As you nibble your goodies, suggest people to invite to Fun Family Night, including kids from Sunday school, neighbors, schoolmates, co-workers of their parents, and other relatives, plus their families. Tell kids to ask their parents' permission, then add the dates and times of Family Fun Night to the invitations. Mail or deliver the invitations in person and get ready for some good, old-fashioned fun and togetherness!

KINDNESS COUNTS

A group of Boy Scouts in California decided to put their skills to work to serve children they didn't even know! The boys began a "toy hospital" to fix and repair worn, broken, or neglected toys. With a bit of elbow grease, a touch of paint and sandpaper, and a whole lotta love, the boys managed to repair over fifty toys to mail to children in poor countries!

SERVICE SALE

God uses us to help others.

Service Scripture: Psalm 103:13; Romans 12:13

GET READY...

This unusual donation-oriented service project to help needy parents of small children can be planned to last several weeks. You'll need to place an ad in the "garage sale" section of your newspaper (usually free for community service projects). You'll also need a Bible, index cards, markers and crayons, an assortment of boxes to decorate, tape, scissors, and baby or juvenile gift wrap.

GET SET...

Have kids form two lines at one end of the room. At the opposite end, place two boxes. Explain that in this relay, the first person in each line must hop to get a box, then hop back to her line and pass the box over her head to the next person. That person will pass the box under his legs and so on in and over-and-under pattern down the line. The last person in line can shout, "Thanks for the help, team!" After the relay, set the boxes aside and ask:

- ⚄ **How did everyone on the team help get the box to the last person in line?**
- ⚄ **In what ways is this like the way God uses us to help others?**
- ⚄ **Why does God want us to serve him by serving others?**
- ⚄ **How does serving God demonstrate obedience? love?**

Read aloud Psalm 103:13 and Romans 12:13, then explain that God often calls us to help others. Point out that God loves his children and knows what they need. Tell kids that God likes to give us wonderful opportunities to help and serve others—and to exercise our love!

Explain that today you'll help provide for the needs of God's children by collecting used toys, clothing, and baby items and placing them in decorated boxes.

GO SERVE!

Let kids work in pairs or trios to decorate and wrap the sides of the boxes. (Keep them open to hold your collected items!) Have kids decorate colorful index cards with Psalm 103:13 written on them, then attach the cards to the boxes or to the items as they're collected.

As you work, explain that your collection is like a "reverse garage sale" in which people *bring* items to you instead of *coming* to buy them! Tell kids to spread the news of your project to their friends and families. Then let kids know that you've also placed an ad in the newspaper to let lots of other people know about your project so they can make donations such as toys, books, children's and baby's clothing, and other baby items. Explain that the collected items will be given to a local children's home or family center to help children of needy families. End by offering a prayer for the children you'll help with your project, then go out and spread the word about your reverse garage sale!

43

Serve one another in love ... 'Love your neighbor as yourself.'

FUN FUND-RAISERS

"WHOEVER SERVES ME MUST FOLLOW ME, AND WHERE I AM, MY SERVANT ALSO WILL BE"

John 12:26

FUN FUND-RAISERS

What's the toughest thing next to finding volunteers for Sunday school? Finding funds for projects! There are so many needs and necessities, wants and wishes to be filled in service to God. How can you make fund-raising fun and unique? Simply sample some of the fun ways to raise funds in the following pages! Kids will love the clever fund-raiser crafts and will discover in no time that a little imagination and elbow grease can return great dividends for the kingdom of God! These fund-raisers provide painless yet purposeful ways to collect money, donations of clothing and food, and much more. And the best part? As you raise funds you'll raise your kids' awareness of needs in the community and the world!

SOUPER SUNDAY

Community

God warms our hearts with love.
Service Scripture: John 21:15, 16

GET READY...

Serve up some good, old-fashioned warmth with this "souper" fund-raiser! You'll need a Bible, poster board, markers, disposable bowls and paper plates, plastic spoons, a variety of crackers, several loaves of French or sheepherder's bread, and several large pots of soup, such as chicken noodle or vegetable beef. These can be homemade soups or purchased in jumbo-sized cans. You'll also need the following decorations: balloons, brown paper footballs, and crepe paper in team colors, such as green and yellow or red and white.

Special Note: This mini fund-raiser is perfect for the Sunday before the Super Bowl—or at noon on Super Bowl Sunday itself. Be sure to advertise a week before your event to get everyone in the "team spirit"!

GET SET...

A week or two prior to your planned mini fund-raiser, gather kids and discuss the upcoming Super Bowl game. Ask questions such as "Which teams are playing?" "Why do you think so many people like team games?" and "How are Christians like a big team?" Explain that there are many people in the world—and in your own town—who may be hungry and feel left off the "team." Tell kids that, as Christians, we're part of Jesus' team and can share our blessings with others. Read aloud John 21:15, 16 then discuss why Jesus wants us to be on his team and care for others.

Invite a volunteer to read aloud the Kindness Counts story from page 48. Then tell kids you have a super way to serve others on Super Bowl Sunday and raise donations for a local food pantry at the same time. Explain that you'll host your own Souper Sunday Supper of soup and other goodies. Attendees will each bring a can of soup or box of crackers with a dollar taped to the label in exchange for a bowl of hot, yummy soup and crackers.

Invite kids to form teams and hand each team a sheet of poster board. Challenge kids to use markers to create "souper" posters advertising your upcoming fund-raiser. Be sure kids tell when the Souper Supper is to be held and that tickets consist of a can of soup or box of crackers and one dollar. Hang the posters in your church or around town, then inform kids when they need to be at the church to help prepare and serve your Souper Supper. For extra fund-raising festivities, plan on holding a drawing for inexpensive footballs, pennants, or team T-shirts.

Whoever serves me must follow me, and where I am, my servant also will be.

47

GO SERVE!

On the day of your event, have teams of kids pitch in to help. One team can stir soup, one can set tables, another can decorate the room, and another may collect cans and donations at the door—with big thank-yous! To make whimsical football bread, simply place French bread or round sheepherder's bread on a plate and use chocolate tube icing to add edible leather laces. What a treat to eat! Twist crepe-paper streamers down the centers of the tables and consider using real footballs as centerpieces!

Sometime during your Souper Supper, ask a child to read aloud the Kindness Counts story, then offer a prayer of thanksgiving for the donations and for the people who will benefit from your fund-raiser. End by leading everyone in this team cheer:

We serve Jesus, and we're so proud,
We just have to shout out loud: We love Jesus!

KINDNESS COUNTS

It pays to listen to your own prayers, a South Carolina minister learned several years ago. After Brad Smith prayed "on this Super Bowl Sunday that we remember those without even a bowl of soup," he came up with an idea that has spread across the country. Why not ask worshipers to give $1 on Super Bowl Sunday to buy soup for the hungry in their own cities? In just a few years, his project has mushroomed to include over 8,600 churches and $1.7 million in collections! Way to go! What a simply "souper" way to serve!

DOGGIE WASH

Community

God loves all of his creation.

Service Scripture: Genesis 1:1-31

GET READY...

This great fund-raiser will raise proceeds that can be donated to a local animal shelter to help even the most helpless of God's creation! For this quick and sudsy fund-raiser, you'll need a warm sunny day, poster board and markers, buckets, a garden hose, plenty of old towels, and no-tears baby shampoo. You'll also want several adults or youth volunteers to help out. If you're really into helping our furry friends, let kids prepare homemade doggie treats. (See the recipe below.)

GET SET...

Have kids name what God created on each of the six days of creation as told in Genesis 1:1-31. Ask kids how each portion of creation shows God's love and how we can care for each. Then invite kids to tell about favorite animals or pets they may have. Ask:

- **How do our pets demonstrate God's love to us?**
- **In what ways does caring for a pet demonstrate our own love and care?**

Remind kids that many animals aren't fortunate enough to have loving homes and must stay in shelters until they're adopted. Explain that animal shelters often run low on food and money to help God's animals and that they can help through a fun fund-raiser. Tell kids you'll hold a dynamite doggie wash (and pet bake sale, if you've chosen to make pet treats).

GO SERVE!

Choose a Saturday or Sunday afternoon to host your event, then have kids make posters to advertise your doggie wash. Be sure to note

Whoever serves me must follow me, and where I am, my servant also will be.

the price ($1 per wash is suggested), the date and time, where your proceeds will go, and that adults must accompany their "furry friends."

On wash day, set up three or four wash stations, making sure a hose is available to fill buckets. At each station, place a bucket, a bottle of no-tears baby shampoo, and plenty of old towels. (Plan on donating some or all of the towels to the animal shelter, too!) Have adults hold their furry friends as you wet them with water from the buckets. Lather the pooches (steer clear of their faces!) and talk sweetly to them—even pets enjoy kind, encouraging words! Rinse off the dogs, then towel dry them. Spread damp towels in the sun to dry.

If you also want to sell doggie treats, use the following recipe and place two treats in plastic bags tied with ribbons or yarn. Sell the treats for $.25 a bag.

Mix 1¼ cup oatmeal, ¼ cup vegetable oil (or oil from tuna to make treats for kitties), and 3 cups beef bouillon. Mix the ingredients until they form a dough. Pinch off pieces of dough or make sausage, fish, or bone shapes from small pieces of dough, then place them on cookie sheets. Bake at 350 degrees for 30 minutes, then cool and place in plastic bags. Woofin' good! Take any unsold treats to the animal shelter as part of your delightful donations!

CALL IT A WRAP!

Church/ Friends

God covers us in love!

Service Scripture: Psalm 91:4, 14

GET READY...

For this useful and festive fund-raiser, you'll need a Bible, packages of colored tissue paper, brown paper bags, scissors, curling ribbon, glue, markers, index cards, a roll of white shelf paper, newspapers, and a variety of craft items, including tempera paints, bingo daubers, stampers and colored ink pads, lace, buttons, and satin ribbon.

GET SET...

Remind kids that God is our Father and covers us with many things, including his protection. Invite kids to brainstorm other things God covers us with, such as his love, truth, power, mercy, and grace. Read aloud Psalm 91:4, 14, then ask:

- ✺ **How does it help to know that God covers us with so much love and other good things?**
- ✺ **In what ways does knowing that God covers us strengthen our faith? our courage? our love?**
- ✺ **How is reminding others of God's covering power a good way to serve them? encourage them? draw them closer to God?**

Tell kids that every day God covers us in a multitude of ways and that we want to serve God and others by reminding them of this wonderful fact! Explain that you'll make colorful gift wrap and package decorations to remind others of how God wraps us in his love!

GO SERVE!

Cover tables with newspapers and set out the bags, shelf paper, and other craft items. You may wish to use three tables and designate one as the flat gift wrap table, one as the decorated gift bags table, and the other as the gift cards table. For flat wrap, have kids cut 2-foot lengths of white shelf paper and decorate the sheets using paint and bingo daubers. (Consider using toothbrushes and sponges instead of paintbrushes to add cool effects and textures!) To decorate gift bags, use bingo daubers, bits of lace, curling and satin ribbon, and buttons. For gift cards, fold index cards in half and use markers, stampers, and bits of lace and ribbon to decorate the fronts.

When everything is decorated, place a sheet of gift wrap, two cards, and several sheets of tissue paper in each decorated gift bag (to wrap two presents). These delightful gift wraps will make gift wrapping a snap—and add a warm, personal touch to any present! Sell the bags for $1 each at a table set up in the church entryway or let kids sell

Whoever serves me must follow me, and where I am, my servant also will be.

their projects to family and friends. Be sure you've chosen a place for your donations to be given, such as to the church for a special project, to a disabled group, or to a local service agency that helps cover others in love!

TEA FOR TWO!

We can help feed the hungry.
Service Scripture: Luke 3:11; John 21:17

GET READY...

This delightful tea will not only bring smiles to the faces of attendees but will also bring smiles to hungry tummies in your community! This fund-raiser will take one day of planning and preparation and can be held after church or during midweek services. Be sure to advertise your fund-raising event in advance!

Today you'll prepare posters and invitations for church members, their families, and friends. You'll also be making the tea and cookies to serve. For this portion, you'll need a Bible, markers, poster board, butter cookies, canned icing, candy sprinkles, plastic knives, paper plates, sugar, unsweetened instant tea, orange gelatin mix, measuring cups, a large spoon and mixing bowl, and copies of the invitation on page 122 (to hand to the congregation). Make one copy of the invitation and fill in the date and time of your party before photocopying the rest of the invitations!

Tea for two or three or four—
When we share with others, love multiplies more!

COME TO OUR TEA PARTY!

WHEN:
WHERE:
COST: $1 or 2 cans of food (All proceeds and donations will go to a local food pantry!)

GET SET...

Set the invitations, markers, and poster board on one table; the cookies, icing, plastic knives, candy sprinkles, and paper plates on a second table; and the tea, sugar, gelatin, measuring cups, mixing bowl, and spoon on a third table.

Gather kids and read aloud John 21:17 and Luke 3:11, then ask:

- **What do think Jesus meant when he told Peter to "feed my sheep"?**
- **In what different ways can we feed someone? For example, we can feed someone food or even love. What others ways can we nourish or feed others?**

Allow time for answers, then explain that there are many ways to be hungry and be fed. One way is to hunger for God's Truth and to nourish someone's spirit with the good things that come from God's Word. Another way is to nourish people's hearts with the good things found in love. Still another way is to feed someone's body through sharing food. Explain that the Lord wants us to help feed the hungry in whatever way we can. Tell kids that this cool fund-raiser will be used to help feed people in your community who are hungry for food—and maybe hungry for a bit of love, too! Explain that you'll host a tea party to raise money to help a local food pantry purchase food.

Go SERVE!

Have kids form three groups: the poster preparers, the cookie creators, and the tea team. Challenge the poster preparers to make several posters advertising your event. Tell them to use the invitations as a guide. Then let those same kids decorate the invitations to be handed out after church. Have the cookie creators decorate butter cookies and place them on paper plates to be served at your tea party. Finally, invite the tea team to prepare the instant tea mix that will be stirred into cups of hot water at your event. Use the following recipe to prepare the tea.

To make approximately twenty cups of tea, mix 2 cups of instant tea, 1 cup of sugar, and two packages of powdered orange gelatin in a large bowl. (Make more according to how many people you think will attend your party.) At party time, simply mix 2 tablespoons in a cup of hot water!

Hand the invitations out after church as the congregation is leaving. During the tea party, offer a prayer for those who are hungry in different ways and for God's help in serving those needs. Then be sure to thank your guests for attending after the tea party!

PRAYER PaGERS

Church

We can serve by praying for others.

Service Scripture: John 17:9; 1 Thessalonians 5:17

GET READY...

This unusual fund-raiser will work wonders for people who may be sick, sad, or otherwise needing special prayers! The point of this unique fund-raiser is to raise enough funds to purchase a Prayer Pager and a year's worth of pager service. (This service is usually about $70, and the pager is free. Check this out in advance so you know how much money to collect!) The Prayer Pager will be given to someone needing special prayers. Whenever this person is prayed for, the pager number is dialed as a reminder that someone in praying for him or her at that very moment! (Neat, isn't it?) When the prayer crisis is over, the Prayer Pager can be given to the next person needing a special reminder of God's—and your kids'—love!

Plan on collecting donations over the next several weeks and ask the leader of the congregation if the kids can make special announcements and reminders of their project each week. Who knows? If people respond in a very generous way, you may be able to purchase two or more Prayer Pagers!

For this week's segment, you'll need a Bible, a pager, a large box, black and white construction paper, tape, scissors, rubber bands, ribbon, crayons, copy paper, and markers. For a wonderful extra touch, consider using pages from a worn-out Bible and hand out the pages as reminders of the precious "prayer pages" someone can receive through your loving fund-raiser!

GET SET...

Invite kids to tell about times they prayed for someone or someone prayed for them. Then read aloud John 17:9a and 1 Thessalonians 5:17 and ask:

Whoever serves me must follow me, and where I am, my servant also will be.

- **How are prayers for others ways to cover them in love?**
- **Why is it important to pray for others?**
- **How does it help to know someone is praying for you? How does it encourage you?**

Hold up the pager and explain how a pager works. Tell kids a pager is a great way to let someone know you're thinking of them. Explain the wonderful Prayer Pager fund-raiser you're about to embark upon. Remind kids that God wants us to pray for others and that a Prayer Pager is a special way to let those with special needs know that someone is thinking about them and praying for them! Tell kids that you'll also make prayer presents to sell during your fund-raiser.

GO SERVE!

Form two groups and designate one group the prayer scribes and the other group the pager decorators. Let the prayer scribes write brief prayers, using favorite Scripture verses or Psalms. Roll each prayer into a scroll and place a rubber band around it, then tie a ribbon around the scroll. These little prayer scrolls can be sold for $.50 each and the donations added to your pager fund. (Keep plenty of scrolls on hand to sell to families, friends, and church members!)

Have the pager decorators decorate a box (the larger the better!) to resemble a real pager. Cover the box in black paper; use the white paper and crayons to add pager features and buttons. You'll also want to add white lines dividing the box into four portions. This will be used much like a thermometer. During the fund-raising, add a strip of red paper as you reach donations that equal the first fourth of your needed cost. Keep adding red paper as your donations increase so the kids and whole congregation can see how close you are to your goal!

When the donations have reached your goal, have kids make lovely thank-you notes for the congregation and hand them out after church. When you first give someone the Prayer Pager, choose several people to receive the pager number (if it's okay with the recipient!). Then, when someone prays for that person, the number can be called as a powerful prayer reminder! What a blessing for people who are sick in the hospital or confined to beds at home! Be sure to pass your Prayer Pager around as it's needed.

Whoever serves me must follow me, and where I am, my servant also will be.

FAST FUND-RAISERS

The following ideas are not only fund-raising—they're fun raising! Perfect for any needs, wants, or concerns, these ideas are quick, easy, and filled with serving fun!

ART AUCTION

Kids will have a wonderful time creating cool pieces of art to auction after a Sunday service! Set out a wide variety of craft and art materials and invite kids to use their gifts and talents creating paintings, clay sculptures, wood creations, tie-dyed fabrics, wearable art, clever craft creations, or any other items within kids' imaginations! (If you want a larger auction, have each child create several items or challenge the youth group to join in the fun!) After church services on a designated day or evening, have a church leader or member of the youth group act as auctioneer. Begin bidding on your delightful works of art at $.25 and raise bids by $.25 increments (more if the items are very large). You'll be surprised at how much fun is created from the unique creations being auctioned!

SCRIPTURE YARD SIGNS

These cool and clever yard signs let everyone know where your love and faith lie, and kids adore making these special messages to display in yards, gardens, and around the church! For each sign, you'll need two paint stir sticks (available from most decorating centers), duct tape, poster board, large markers, crepe paper, tape, and balloons. Cut sheets of poster board in half and decorate one side with simple phrases such as "God is in control!" (Psalm 24:1), "Jesus loves us!" (Romans 8:39), "Forgive one another!" (Colossians 3:13), "Encourage someone today!" (Ephesians 4:32), and "Help a friend today!" (Galatians 5:22). Add Scripture references after each phrase. Tape one stir stick horizontally across the back of each sign and tape another stick vertically to be stuck in the ground. Have each child make two or three signs.

Sell your cheery greetings to family, friends, and church members for a suggested price of $1 each or a whole set at a discounted price!

COOKiE POPS

These delicious treats are a favorite with kids—both making and eating them! For each cookie pop, spread icing between two chocolate chip cookies. Slide a new craft stick between the cookies. Decorate one or both sides of the cookies with squeeze icing and tiny candies. Slip each cookie pop in a plastic sandwich bag and tie a ribbon bow beneath each cookie. Suggested sale price: $.50 a pop. (For even more fun, take orders and personalize the cookie pops for birthdays, holidays, or other special times!)

KiNDNESS COUNTS

Miracles can happen. Just ask a boy from Tijuana, Mexico, who was helped by the prayers and proceeds of a group of Sunday school kids in Colorado. These kids learned of the boy's rare illness and how he needed surgery, but his family could not afford it. Through the kids' prayers and a series of small fund-raisers, the boy was flown to the United States, where doctors and hospital staff donated their services to treat the boy.

Whoever serves me must follow me, and where I am, my servant also will be.

RECIPES FOR LIFE

Have kids write recipes based on Galatians 5:22, 23 for love, joy, peace, patience, kindness, goodness, faithfulness, gentleness, and self-control. Be sure to have each child sign his recipes! Copy and collate these special recipes into books with covers made of construction paper or wallpaper from wallpaper sample books (available at decorating stores). These books make precious keepsakes for parents and grandparents and can be sold for $1 a book or discounted for multiple copies!

SUPER-STORE

Check with companies and mail-order houses such as the Oriental Trading Company (see the Service Directory) for adorable items to sell at very reasonable prices. Many of these catalog houses also carry clever Christian items! You can purchase a wonderful variety of items in bulk for a fraction of the retail price and let kids select which items they might like to sell at several Super-Store Sundays. Simply price the items and set them on display tables. Let kids act as bookkeepers, cashiers, and inventory managers. Designate a worthy cause for your profits. Advertise well in advance and let your shoppers know where a portion of their purchase is going! Kids will gain useful experience shopkeeping, pricing, bookkeeping, and figuring costs, in addition to providing help for a local charity or service program!

SECRET SCRIPTURE SOAP BALLS

According to Psalm 119:11, we're to hide God's Word in our hearts. But how about hiding God's Word in soap balls for a bit of "clean" Bible fun? Have kids cut 1-inch by ½-inch pieces of plastic from empty milk jugs, then use fine-tipped permanent markers to write Bible references such as Galatians 5:13, John 3:16, Ephesians 4:32, and Philippians 4:13 on the plastic strips. Then help kids whip six cups of soap flakes with enough water to make a stiff "dough." Form the soap balls around the pieces of plastic so the soap balls are about the size of golf balls. Set the soap balls on waxed paper to dry for several days, then place them in plastic sandwich bags and sell your secret soap balls for $.50 apiece. What a great way to get clean and learn God's Word at the same time!

COOL CLIPS

Want a cool way to collect donations? Make money clips and exchange the "fun" money in these cool clips for real donations. For each clip, you'll need a copy of the dollar bill below (copy the dollars on green paper for a more realistic effect), medium-sized binder clips (available at office supply stores), and gold or silver metallic paint pens. Use the pens to paint cool designs on the clips. When the paint dries, cut out the dollars and clip them to the money clips. Sell the money clips to members of the congregation, family, and friends for whatever someone is able to donate, or exchange the money clip and dollar for a real dollar bill. (These clips are great grocery-list holders, note holders when hung on a wall, or even desk clips for that special someone's office!)

SPOON LOLLIES

These neat treats are perfect to nibble and delightful to stir into cups of tea or coffee. In other words, everyone will love these festive fund-raisers and clamor for more! To make a set of six spoons, simply have kids dip plastic spoons in melted chocolate. Use dark chocolate for one spoon in the set, milk chocolate for two spoons, and add drops of mint or cherry flavoring in the chocolate before dipping the last spoons. Place the coated spoons on waxed paper to harden, then slip six spoons in a plastic sandwich bag and tie the handles together with ribbon. You may wish to attach a note saying, "Great to lick like a lolly-on-a-stick, or stir them in coffee or tea for a treat that's slick!" Sell each set of tasty treats for $.50. These make wonderful Mother's Day or Father's Day gifts, too!

KiNDNESS COUNTS

A ten-year-old girl in Chicago was touched by the tragedy of a family losing all they had in a fire. This clever girl decided to "get hopping" and serve in an unusual way! She recruited her family and friends and hosted a jump-rope-a-thon to raise money to help the family. The event was covered by local television stations and newspapers, and many people from all over the Chicago area turned out to turn the ropes and hop to help!

MərVELÖUS MISSIÖNS

"THERE ARE DIFFERENT KINDS OF SERVICE, BUT THE SAME LORD."

1 Corinthians 12:5

MaRVELOUS MISSIONS!

Missions are perhaps the toughest thing to teach kids about. *What is a missionary? Why do missionaries have to travel so far? How do missionaries receive funding and make a living as they serve God?* Help your kids learn about the important roles of missionaries as they do their part to serve these special servants of God. In this section, you'll discover a wonderful variety of ways to support, encourage, and thank missionaries around the world or around the corner! Most of these projects can be completed with a minimum of time, and all use simple-to-find supplies. Whether offering postcard vacations or buying goats for a village halfway around the world, kids will have the opportunity to explore missions and what their time and talents can do to help further the kingdom of God—without leaving home!

give a goat!

World Missions

Serving is as fun as it is helpful!
Service Scripture: 2 Corinthians 9:7

GET READY...

Here's a service project kids will remember forever—and so will people in another part of the world! You'll need a Bible, a world atlas or large wall map, markers, scissors, envelopes, glue, a photocopy of the goat in the margin for each child, and colorful

photocopies of the Care Card on page 123. You'll need five cards for each child.

Special Note: This unique missions-based project takes several weeks to complete—but it's worth the wait! You'll want to contact Heifer Project International at 1-800-422-0474 prior to your missions project to determine the price of purchasing a goat for a village. The price is much less than you'd think! (See the Kindness Counts information on page 64.) Check out which country you'll be helping and share this information with your kids to bring your project closer to home!

GET SET... ᥫ ᥫ ᥫ

Hold up the world atlas and invite volunteers to point out the locations of disadvantaged countries such as India, Pakistan, or Kenya and Somalia in Africa. Explain that these countries are so poor that many of the villages have few if any animals to help feed and clothe the people who live there. Discuss what it would be like to live without clean water to drink, fresh clothes to wear, and food to eat. Explain that Jesus uses people who have much to share with those who have little. Read aloud 2 Corinthians 9:7, then ask:

ᥫ **How does giving to others make us happy? make God happy?**

ᥫ **Why does Jesus want us to share our blessings?**

ᥫ **How is sharing a way to serve God? strengthen our faith?**

Have kids form groups of two or four and brainstorm what things a village goat or cow could provide. When you're done, ask groups to share their ideas with the class. Ask children if they'd like to purchase a goat for a village. Explain that they'll go to their families, friends, neighbors, and church members to ask if they would like to pitch in money to purchase a goat for a poor village. Then hand each child a copy of the goat illustration and an envelope. Glue the paper goats to the envelopes, then color and decorate them. These will be donation envelopes.

GO SERVE!

As children are decorating their envelopes, suggest clever "selling techniques" kids can use. For example, suggest to prospective donors that a goat would make a unique birthday gift for someone special and could even be named in honor of the birthday person! If donors choose to "give a goat," kids collect the money, then present the donor with a photocopied Care Card to present to their special someone. Donations may be anywhere from $1 on up. Allow several weeks or a month to complete your Give a Goat campaign. Be sure to provide as many gift cards as kids need!

When enough money is collected to purchase at least one goat, hold a simple celebration—serve crackers and goat cheese. Place the donation envelopes in one large envelope, then offer a prayer for the village who will receive your gift of love.

If your kids enjoyed this cool missions project, consider "wrapping up a rooster," "presenting a pig," "bestowing honey bees," or even "collecting a cow"! The difference you make will last a lifetime!

KINDNESS COUNTS

Heifer Project International provides a variety of livestock to poor families in 110 countries around the world. These animals provide eggs, milk, and cheese for many needy families to eat. A gift of about $20 can purchase a whole flock of chickens for a poor village! And check out Heifer Project's Fill the Ark program for a whole church or community drive—it's an ark full of fun! Call Heifer Project International for more details. (See Service Directory.)

OATMEAL-A-THON

God wants us to share what we have.

Service Scripture: Luke 3:11

GET READY...

This mini missions project can be focused to serve local food pantries or homeless shelters, or it can be used to raise money to help feed the hungry in another country. For example, did you know that for only about $7 you can feed a hungry Russian child hot meals for an entire week?

Plan on hosting an Oatmeal-a-Thon breakfast one Sunday. For this wonderful church-family meal, provide flavored, instant stir-n-serve oatmeal packets; hot water; chilled juice; donut holes; paper bowls; napkins; and cups. You'll also need resealable plastic bags, instant oats, brown sugar, cinnamon, index cards, markers, tape, and plastic spoons.

GET SET...

Invite kids to tell about times they might have felt really hungry and how long they had to wait to eat. Then challenge kids to think about what it would be like never to have a favorite food or only to eat one meal a day or even a week. Point out that we are very blessed to never wait long when we're hungry but that some people are not so lucky and even go to bed hungry every night. Tell children that hunger affects not only our bodies but also the way we think, act, and sleep. Without enough food, it's impossible to do many things for ourselves and to think about anything other than our hunger. Read aloud Luke 3:11, then ask:

- **How does hunger keep people from helping themselves? from serving God? from learning about God?**
- **Why do you think God wants us to share what we have— even our food—with others?**
- **In what ways does feeding the hungry help draw those people closer to God?**

There are different kinds of service, but the same Lord.

Explain that your missionary project for the next several days (or weeks) will be to help feed the hungry, to share what you have, and to encourage others to find God. Tell kids that you'll host a delicious Oatmeal-a-Thon to encourage others to think about hunger and helping. Explain your plans for the oatmeal breakfast, then tell kids that today they'll prepare bags of yummy instant oatmeal to sell.

Go Serve!

Help kids prepare resealable bags to make "instant breakfasts." In each bag, place ¾ cup instant oats, 2 plastic spoonfuls of brown sugar, and 1 spoonful of cinnamon. Seal the bags and tape on cards with the words to Luke 3:11 written on them. Challenge families, friends, and church members to purchase an instant breakfast bag for each family member (at a suggested price of $.50 or $1) to enjoy and to remind them that serving God includes sharing the good things we have with others in need. Remind everyone that what is spare change for many of us can mean the difference between eating and starving for someone else! Collect the sales money in an empty oatmeal container. Consider donating your funds to Hot Meals, a division of Samaritan's Purse devoted to helping feed hungry people around the world. (See the Service Directory for more information.)

On the morning of your Oatmeal-a-Thon breakfast, provide bowls of instant, flavored oatmeal and hot water so participants in the congregation can make their own delicious breakfasts. Add chilled juice and donut holes and charge $1.50 per person, with proceeds going to help a local food-service agency. Be sure to have kids tell a bit about world and local hunger and why God wants us to share our blessings with those in need. Read Isaiah 58:7 and John 21:17 for good reminders of feeding the lambs whom God loves. Then close by offering a prayer asking God's blessing on your food and on the donations you're collecting to help feed others.

BUILD A HOUSE

We can work together to build good things.

Service Scripture: 1 Corinthians 3:11

GET READY...

This service project is a hands-on one kids will love! You'll be building unusual birdhouses and use them to collect donations for missions-sponsored building projects abroad or for a service agency such as Habitat for Humanity, which helps build houses for the needy worldwide. (See Service Directory.)

For this project, you'll need duct tape, tacky craft glue, tempera paint, lace, ribbons, buttons, sequins, feathers and fake fur, and empty containers such as cans, boxes, large soda-pop bottles, milk jugs, and small wooden crates. (Steer clear of glass containers.) Be sure you have one container for each child plus a few extras to give kids a choice of what to build their houses out of! You'll also want to get permission from your church leader to let kids explain to the congregation their missions project and how they're collecting funds to help build houses and churches.

GET SET...

Set out the craft materials, then gather kids and invite them to tell about their homes or places they've lived. Encourage kids to tell what it feels like to have a special place they call home, whether it's a house, apartment, or condominium. Read aloud 1 Corinthians 3:11, then ask:

- **In what ways is Jesus the perfect foundation for our lives?**
- **How does serving Jesus strengthen our foundation of faith?**
- **Why is it important to help others build homes and churches? foundations of faith?**

Explain that many people in the world don't have good, safe, solid places to live or worship. Point out that many of these same people

There are different kinds of service, but the same Lord.

have no foundation of faith because they don't know the Lord. Tell kids that missionaries help villagers and other people build their lives on Jesus while helping build places to live or churches in which to worship. Then explain that kids can help with missionaries' building projects by doing a bit of building on a smaller scale.

Tell kids that they'll be making cool miniature houses to collect donations for building projects. When the project is done helping provide houses for people, the small houses will be donated for our feathered friends to live in!

GO SERVE!

Let kids work in small groups to build their houses. Have everyone choose a container with which to build a house, then use the various craft items to create a "dream home." As kids work, have them tell favorite things about homes they've lived in. Remind kids that a great way to serve is to help people build, repair, or care for their homes when they're unable to do it alone.

When the houses are complete, have kids display their creations. Then have children explain to the congregation what their service project is about and how they're raising funds to build new houses and churches locally and abroad through missions. Read aloud 1 Corinthians 3:11, then lead the congregation in a prayer asking God to bless your project and the people who will live in the houses and worship in the churches your funds help to build. Place the houses on a table in the church entryway and let people make donations for the next several weeks. Place a sign on the table that says, "Building lives and homes in Christ!"

When your building project is completed, be sure to thank everyone for their loving help. Then let kids hang their small houses in trees or bushes as cozy homes for birds!

MINI MISSIONS

The following ideas are marvelous missions ideas to help a variety of missionaries, missions agencies, and local missions projects. These ideas are all quick, easy, filled with fun, and leave you with no excuse *not* to jump into the missions field to serve! Remember to advertise and promote your missions projects to give others the opportunity to help and donate. Remind kids that many people want to help, they just aren't sure how. But when a great missions project comes along, they're delighted to donate, eager to help, and enjoy joining in the fun of serving others for God! Remember: "The harvest is plentiful but the workers are few"—so encourage others to get out there and go for God!

BOOKPLATES FOR BIBLES

Have kids create bookplates for the insides of Bibles from large self-adhesive labels. Before letting kids decorate the labels, have them write on the label:

This Bible could belong to a child in _____ .
Donation by the _____ *family.*

Use permanent markers, stampers and ink, or colored pens to decorate the labels. Have kids fill in the names of countries (use an atlas if necessary), then add hearts, stars, and other designs to the labels. Get permission from church leaders to "sell" the bookplates for the cost of a Bible to be sent to another country. (For example, $10 can supply a Bible for a child or adult in Sri Lanka. See Samaritan's Purse in the Service Directory.)

Ask for permission to affix the bookplates in Bibles or hymnals in the pews whenever someone purchases them. Then write the names of the purchasers or their family names on the name blanks of the bookplates and place them in the front of a Bible or hymnal set in the church pews. What a lovely gift a family can make in the name of a

There are different kinds of service, but the same Lord.

loved one! (If you'll affix bookplates to hymnals in the pews, make bookplates that say *hymnal* rather than *Bible*.)

STUCK ON STICKERS

Here's a quick-n-easy missions project that your church-sponsored missionaries will really get "stuck" on! Ask kids to collect sheets and packages of self-adhesive stickers and place them in a large decorated envelope to send to church-sponsored missionaries. The stickers are a treasured treat in disadvantaged areas or with kids in foreign countries who may have never received stickers before! Choose stickers that have biblical themes, animals, heart shapes, flowers, or other cheerful illustrations. Avoid super-hero type stickers or ones that show cartoon characters. For an extra treat, send lengths or bolts of colorful ribbon that can be cut to make pretty bookmarks with stickers on the ends. Even the smallest items bring loads of cheer, love, and encouragement!

KINDNESS COUNTS

More than forty-five families and friends in the Midwest worked together to "stomp" out world hunger. A group of kids in a local church decided to host a Hike-for-Hunger event and asked sponsors to donate one dollar for each mile walked. Many churches in the area joined in, and by the end of the hike, several thousand dollars had been collected to give to CROP (Christian Rural Overseas Program; see Service Directory) to help feed hungry people in third-world countries. We can all get "in step" to serve!

FiELD SEWiNG KiTS

These great little sewing kits are as fun to make as they are useful to field missionaries or even members of the military. For each mini sewing kit, you'll need a small or medium sliding matchbox, six buttons, felt, several safety pins, several needles, cardboard, and colored thread. To assemble a kit, cover the outside of the matchbox with felt, gluing it in place with tacky craft glue. Glue the felt so the ends barely meet on the bottom and don't overlap. Glue two or three buttons to the top. As the glue dries, cut a small piece of cardboard to fit inside the box. Wrap thread around the cardboard. Cut a small piece of felt to fit inside the box and slide the needles into the felt, then pin a few safety pins to the piece of felt. Slide the thread and needles and pins into the bottom of the matchbox and place three buttons inside. Isn't this idea "sew" neat?

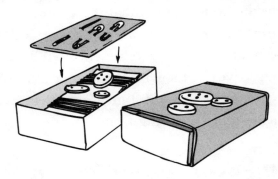

GREAT GAMES BOX

This cool missions project will be as appreciated in a foreign country as in a missions field close to home! Let kids work to assemble a box filled with items that can be used to play a wide variety of games. Include donated balloons, playground balls, paddles, jigsaw puzzles, flying rings, plastic cups, a colorful beach ball, bandanas and bean bags, and any other game items your kids can brainstorm. Assemble your "shopping list" into a scavenger hunt list and let kids gather the items. Then challenge kids to form small groups and invent games with simple rules that use these playing props. Games that might spark cool rules could be balloon badminton, plastic-cup relays, or beachball volleyball. Have kids write their games (along with any game diagrams) on paper, then decorate the pages. Assemble the pages in a game book to copy and place in a decorated box along with the game items. Keep copies of the item list and games kids invent, then challenge everyone to put together a kit for your own church to use for VBS, church picnics, or family retreats.

71

DOLLARS FOR DISASTERS

This missions project is especially appreciated and blessed after a natural disaster such as a hurricane, flood, earthquake, or tidal wave. Copy the dollar pattern from page 59 on light green paper, then let kids assemble a huge paper tree on a wall where congregation members will see it as they enter and leave the church. Make the tree trunk and branches from twisted brown-paper grocery sacks; tape the trunk and branches to the wall with clear packing tape. Tape the "dollar leaves" to the branches. Cut out colorful paper letters that spell out "The Missions Tree" and tape them beside the tree. Have kids explain to the congregation that these special dollars can be plucked from the tree and replaced with real paper dollars or envelopes containing donations for your relief effort. Tell participants they can keep the dollar leaves in their Bibles as special bookmarks to remind them that God loves a cheerful giver and that together we can turn a natural disaster into a blessing from God!

FRESH FOOTSTEPS

Every field missionary knows how precious soap and laundry detergent are! With this project, kids will have a great time encouraging missionaries to keep in lively "step" as they walk the world to tell others about Jesus. Read aloud Matthew 28:19 and remind kids that Jesus wants us to go into all the world to tell others about his love and forgiveness, which is what missionaries do! Remind kids that missionaries put a lot of miles on their feet taking the gospel around the world and that they can help keep missionaries' feet fresh and ready to keep going.

You'll need a new pair of socks (men's or women's) for each child, a box of powdered laundry detergent (for missionaries to wash their socks and other clothes), and a box of mineral salts (to soak missionaries' tired feet). You'll also need markers, index cards, a paper punch, and rubber bands.

For each pair of socks, pour ½ cup of laundry detergent in one sock and mineral salts in the other. Write the words *detergent* and *foot bath* on index cards and attach them securely to the appropriate socks with rubber bands. Finally, use a rubber band to hold the socks together as a pair. Send the socks to your church-sponsored missionaries, or you may even give them to a homeless shelter for a local service project!

POSTCARD VACATION

Send your church-sponsored missionaries on a relaxing "vacation" via colorful, scenic postcards! Have kids collect postcards from your area or draw their favorite scenes on large index cards. On the backs of the postcards or index cards, invite kids to write cheery, encouraging notes to the missionaries, making sure to thank them for the wonderful work they're doing in the name of the Lord. Kids may want to include a favorite Scripture verse, jokes or riddles, and information about themselves so missionaries' kids can get to know their long-distance postcard pals! Send the postcards in a bright envelope to the missionaries and their families.

KINDNESS COUNTS

A church in southern Texas got everyone into the act to kick off the school year by assembling backpacks filled with school supplies for kids in homeless shelters. The church sent home flyers asking parents and kids to purchase two of everything they were getting for their own back-to-school needs, including paper, pencils, erasers, notebooks, and folders. Adults pledged to each purchase one empty backpack. At a back-to-school party, everyone packed the packs full of goodies and school supplies. What a great lesson in serving!

There are different kinds of service, but the same Lord.

HOLIDAY HELPS

"AS WE HAVE OPPORTUNITY, LET US DO GOOD TO ALL PEOPLE."

Galatians 6:10

HOLIDAY HELPS

Hustle-bustle holidays are tough times of year for many people. From working moms and dads to lonely seniors, lots of people need a lift during holidays. These quick-n-easy service projects can turn any holiday into a happy happening in a snap! All of these projects require only one class session to complete and touch the lives of countless people, from the teens in your church to family, friends, and others in the community. Sprinkle these special projects generously throughout the year and make this year the most service- and celebration-oriented year in your kids' lives!

A REAL BLOWOUT!

Family/ Friends

New Year's: Jesus helps us change!
Service Scripture: 2 Corinthians 5:17

GET READY...

You'll need a Bible, fine-tipped permanent markers in various colors, and plenty of plain-colored party blowouts, horns, or hats. You can find these items at party supply stores. If you can't find solid-colored items, simply have kids write: "The old has gone, the new has come!" on 2-by-3-inch pieces of construction paper. Then glue the papers to the party items.

GET SET...

Tell kids that New Year's Day is almost here and that it's the time of year when people make resolutions to change and to become like new. Then read aloud 2 Corinthians 5:17. Ask:

- How does Jesus help us change for the better?
- What does it mean to become a new creation in Christ?
- How can loving Jesus help us keep our New Year's resolutions?

Remind kids that whenever we change with Jesus' help, it's like a new year beginning! Explain that you'll make cool New Year's reminders of our new lives in Christ to hand to family members or friends.

GO SERVE!

Have each child choose as many party blowouts, horns, or hats as there are members in her immediate family. Help kids write "The old has gone, the new has come!" on the party items. On the blowouts, write the words on the portion that unfurls, then roll it up again so the message is revealed when the blowout is blown on. Write the words anywhere on the horns and hats.

Encourage children to hand out the party items to family members to remind them to demonstrate the new life that Jesus brings throughout the new year. End by offering a prayer thanking Jesus for our new lives in him and for his love that carries through the new year—and every year after!

EVERY DAY COUNTS!   Family

New Year's: We can serve and pray every day!

Service Scripture: Hebrews 10:24

GET READY...

Kids love having new calendars to color, write on, and count the days with! This cool calendar project will get everyone thinking about ways to serve, pray, and praise during the coming year. You'll need markers, staplers, a paper punch, and enlarged photocopies of the cal-

As we have opportunity, let us do good to all people.

endar page from page 124. Copy twelve of these pages for each child to take home to use with his family. (If you prefer, copy the calendar page on the fronts and backs of six pages—you'll save oodles of paper this way!)

GET SET...

Invite kids to tell ways their families and friends celebrate New Year's. Point out that a new year is a great time to begin a new family tradition of growing closer by praying, serving, and working together. Read aloud Hebrews 10:24, then remind kids that showing kindness, patience, and love every day of the year is important and just how God wants us to be. Explain that your service project today involves making a wonderful family calendar to use throughout the new year.

GO SERVE!

Hand each child a year's worth of blank calendars. Hold up a blank calendar page and show kids where to fill in the name of the month (after "Welcome to . . ."). Read the ways to serve, pray, and spread God's love written in many of the squares. Explain that, when families come to a day when there's something written, the entire family is to do what's suggested. Invite kids to write in the names of the months, then decorate the edges of the calendars with monthly themes, such as flowers for May, hearts for February, and so on. When the pages are complete, compile them in order of the months, then staple the top to make a flip-chart type calendar. If you wish, use a paper punch to add a hole at the top of each calendar so it can be hung on the wall. Encourage kids to have their families brainstorm more ways to serve, show kindness, and pray and write these ideas in the blank squares for each month.

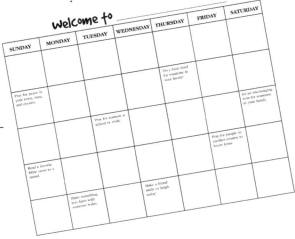

As we have opportunity, let us do good to all people.

BLESS THE BIRDS!

New Year's: God wants us to care for his creation.

Service Scripture: Genesis 1

GET READY...

Get ready to serve some fine feathered friends as you celebrate another new year of God's wonderful creation! You'll need a Bible or Bible storybook, pine cones, peanut butter, scissors, yarn, a paper punch, plastic knives, popped popcorn, birdseed, sunflower seeds, and small disposable plastic plates. You'll also need an undecorated, cut Christmas tree or several real evergreen wreaths. Check local nurseries for their discards or ask members of the congregation to donate their old holiday greenery.

GET SET...

Welcome kids to another new year, then ask kids if they can identify the very first New Year's—God's creation! Read aloud Genesis 1 from a Bible or Bible storybook and have kids identify the six days of creation. Remind kids that after each day of creation, God "saw that it was good." Point out that God created the world from his great love and that we can help care for all of God's creations. Ask:

- ❧ **Why is it important to take care of what God made?**
- ❧ **In what ways does caring for creation demonstrate our love for God? our thanks?**

Explain that today you'll serve a special part of God's creation as you make delightful bird shelters and feeders to care for God's little feathered friends.

GO SERVE!

Show kids how to spread peanut butter on pine cones and paper plates, then roll the sticky items in birdseed, popped popcorn, and

As we have opportunity, let us do good to all people.

sunflower seeds. Tie yarn to the pine cones as hangers. To make paper-plate hangers, simply punch holes in the plates and thread yarn through. Tie the yarn in loops and hang the decorations on the Christmas tree or on several wreaths. Place the Christmas tree in the church yard against a fence or bush so it won't tip over. Hang the wreaths on trees, bushes, or fences. Replenish pine cones and birdseed as needed throughout the winter months.

Finish with a prayer asking God to watch over all the animals of his creation during the cold winter months, when food may be hard to find. Then sit back and enjoy the thankful birds' songs!

HIDE-N-SEEK HEARTS

Family

Valentine's Day: God taught us how to love.

Service Scripture: 1 John 4:7

GET READY...

This crafty reminder of love and laughter is as fun to make as it is to hide! And the best part? This idea serves families throughout the year, not just on Valentine's Day! You'll need a Bible, colored poster board, markers, lace, buttons, scissors, tacky craft glue, and copies of the Hide-n-Seek Valentine poem from page 122.

GET SET...

Read aloud 1 John 4:7, then invite kids to tell about what love and their loved ones mean to them. Ask:

- **In what ways has God taught us what love means and how to love others?**
- **How is loving others a way to show our love for God as well?**
- **Why is it nice to demonstrate our love all year and not just at Valentine's Day?**

⚙ Why is it especially important to tell and show love to our families and other loved ones?

Remind kids that the Bible tells us that the greatest thing we can have is love and that all good things, including kindness, compassion, forgiveness, and serving, come from love. Explain that Valentine's Day is a holiday celebrating love but that the celebration of love isn't just for February 14, it's for every day of our lives! Tell kids you'll make a neat Hide-n-Seek game to play all year long with their families as wonderful reminders of our love from God and our love for family members.

Go SERVE!

Have kids cut out large poster-board hearts and use markers, lace, and buttons to decorate them. Hand each child a copy of the Hide-n-Seek Valentine poem, then ask kids to take turns reading portions of the poem aloud. Explain that these hearts are to be hidden in the house and that whenever a family member finds the special heart, he brings it to the entire family for a loving hug. Then the finder has a turn at hiding the Valentine. Challenge kids to see if their families can keep the fun and loving hugs going all year long!

Hide-n-Seek Valentine

God's love for us is kind and true;
He loves us no matter what we do.
And God wants us to spread wonderful love
As he showers it forth from heaven above!
So use this Valentine heart all year
To keep giving love to those you hold dear.
Hide this heart like Hide-n-Seek
In a place where another person might peek.
And when the heart is finally found,
Give family hugs and love will abound!

"Love one another, for
love comes from God"
(1 John 4:7).

LOViNG REMiNDERS   Community

Valentine's Day: Love carries us through.

Service Scripture: 1 Corinthians 13:4-7

GET READY...

Help those feeling unloved or forgotten remember that God's love helps us bear all things and carries us through even the loneliest times.

As we have opportunity, let us do good to all people.

81

For these adorable Valentine's Day reminders, you'll need a Bible, poster board, yarn, tape, a paper punch, plastic sandwich bags, scissors, markers, and gummy candy bears or teddy bear-shaped cookies.

GET SET...

Set out the craft materials and candy bears. Invite kids to tell about times they may have felt lonely or as though no one cared about them. Then remind kids that when we have love, we can bear all things. Read aloud 1 Corinthians 13:4-7, then ask:

◉ **In what ways is love kind? patient? encouraging?**

◉ **How can knowing someone cares help us through lonely times? fears? sadness?**

Tell kids that many elderly people feel forgotten or lonely. Their own kids have moved away, their friends may be ill, and many older people may not have opportunities to meet other people or go places. Explain that God wants us to remember those people who may feel lonely or forgotten. Tell kids that this service project will remind these people that they are loved and that love "bears" all things.

GO SERVE!

Show kids how to cut two matching hearts from poster board. (You may wish to have poster-board patterns ready for kids to trace and cut.) Punch holes three-fourths of the way around the hearts, then lace yarn through the holes and tie the ends. Decorate the hearts, then write "Love 'bears' all!" on one side and "1 Corinthians 13:4-7" on the other. Fill the poster-board hearts with candy or cookie teddy bears. Finally, slip the hearts and goodies into plastic sandwich bags and tape the bags closed.

Pray that God will remind the recipients of your loving project that they are not forgotten and that God and you care for them! Deliver your special loving treats to a senior care center or homeless shelter.

HEART MATCH-UPS

Valentine's Day: We can greet one another with love.

Service Scripture: Romans 16:16

GET READY...

This instant service project is guaranteed to get people mixing, mingling, and smiling! You'll need a Bible and plenty of bags filled with large candy conversation hearts.

GET SET...

Get permission from your minister to hand out these hearts and use them in a fun way to greet one another either before or at the end of the church service.

Before handing out the candy hearts, have kids read aloud Romans 16:16, then explain that long ago, Christians greeted each other with what was called a "holy kiss," that is, a gentle brush of the lips on another's cheek. Jesus was betrayed by Judas in the same way, so remind kids that the important thing was the heart of love, not the act. Point out that as years wore on, Christians began greeting one another in different ways, such as with handshakes or hearty "hellos." Remind kids that greeting fellow Christians is a warm and wonderful act of Jesus' love and lets others know that we're glad we know them. Tell kids that today's simple service project is to encourage people in church to greet each other, not with holy kisses, but with happy hearts!

GO SERVE!

Have kids hand out the candy hearts to everyone in church. Then invite those having the same color hearts to gather at specified places in the sanctuary or other meeting place. Encourage group members to greet each other with a handshake and a happy "hello." After everyone has been greeted, have two groups join and greet one another. End

As we have opportunity, let us do good to all people.

your time with a brief prayer thanking God for each other and for the ability to greet one another in God's name and Christ's love!

SUN-CLOCKS

Daylight Savings Day: Everything happens in God's time.
Service Scripture: Ecclesiastes 3:1

GET READY...

These too-cool sun-clocks remind us that all things happen in God's will and in his time—and they are also handy reminders of the Daylight Savings Time change! You'll need a Bible, a large coffee can, instant plaster of Paris, water, a sturdy (old) spoon, plastic disposable bowls, dowel rods, crepe paper, markers, scissors, tape, and a variety of rocks, pebbles, and seashells. You'll need one 12-inch length of ½-inch dowel rod for each child.

Special note: Don't be afraid to mix and use plaster of Paris—it's really quite simple! Mix the powder and water in the coffee can according to the directions on the package of plaster. Have the plastic bowls lined up and ready to be half-filled with the plaster. Quick-set plaster of Paris will set up in several minutes and dry completely in about one hour. To remove the plaster garden stone from the bowl, simply pop it out! The plastic won't stick, and you'll have a perfectly round stone!

GET SET...

If the day is sunny, go outdoors to mix and pour the plaster. Read aloud Ecclesiastes 3:1, then ask:

⑥ **Why is God's timing perfect?**

How does it help to know that God is in control of when things happen?

Remind kids that God is in control of everything that happens, so we should trust his timing. Point out that it isn't always easy to wait upon God's timing but that God let's all things happen when they are supposed to. Tell kids that today they will make wonderful garden sun-clocks as reminders for their families that all things happen in God's will and in his time. Explain that these cool clocks will also serve as good reminders of the time change to Daylight Savings Time (if your state observes the time change).

GO SERVE!

Mix the plaster of Paris and pour each plastic bowl half full. When the plaster starts to thicken slightly, let kids gently push pretty rocks, pebbles, and seashells into the plaster in designs around the edges. Then, as the plaster is about set, have kids push dowel rods into the centers of the plaster so they stick as straight up as possible. (These will be the sun dials.)

When the garden sun-clocks are set, pop them out of the plastic bowls and tape lengths of crepe paper from the dowels. On the crepe-paper streamers, write the day that Daylight Savings Time begins in your area. Have kids take them home to their families to either set on a sunny porch or bury at ground level in a garden as a sun-clock. (As the day progresses, the shadow from the dowel will move in an arc.) Encourage kids to remind their families that all things happen in God's time.

As we have opportunity, let us do good to all people.

EggStravaganZa!

Easter: We can proclaim the good news about Jesus!

Service Scripture: Matthew 28:19

GET READY...

This simple, yet simply super, service project is fast and full of fun. You'll need a Bible, plastic pull-apart eggs, paper punches, craft glue, plastic sandwich bags, colorful construction paper, scissors, and fine-tipped markers. If you don't have time for kids to make their own confetti by punching holes in construction paper, simply purchase ready-made confetti from a party supply store.

GET SET...

Have kids form pairs or trios and each tell their partners something about Jesus. Suggestions might include that Jesus loves us, that Jesus died for our sins, that Jesus can forgive us, and that we want to be baptized as Jesus was. Then read aloud Matthew 28:19 and ask:

☙ **How does it serve others when we tell them the good news about Jesus?**

☙ **What things can we tell others about Jesus?**

Remind kids that Jesus told us to go into all the world and baptize others and tell them the good news about his love and forgiveness. Then tell kids that their service project today will tell others about the Lord and his love.

Go SERVE!

Have kids work in their pairs or trios to write messages about Jesus on small slips of construction paper. Then have kids punch out colorful confetti and place it in the sandwich bags. Show kids how to use their fingers to spread the outsides of the pull-apart egg halves with glue, then shake the sticky eggs to coat them with colorful paper bits.

When the egg halves are dry, insert one or two slips of paper containing messages about Jesus, such as "Jesus is alive!" or "Jesus is our Savior!" Hand the eggs to friends at church and ask them to read the messages inside before they pass the eggs to another friend and so on. End by praying for people all over the world to hear and accept the good news about Jesus during this Easter season and throughout the entire year!

EASTER ANGEL

World

Easter: We can encourage others with our love.

Service Scripture: Philippians 1:3-6

GET READY...

These adorable cookies-n-containers will help missionaries celebrate Easter with love. You'll need a Bible, newspapers, assorted colors of icing, tiny assorted candies, powdered sugar, plastic knives, packages of prepared cookies, and wax paper. For each angel cookie jar, you'll need a large plastic jar and lid, white lace, excelsior, tacky craft glue, paints or markers, note cards, fine-tipped markers, and tape.

Special Note: This incredible, edible service project makes a perfect Easter treat for missionaries in other parts of the world, where their favorite cookies may not be available. If you'd like white angel jars, spray paint the plastic jars before this project or purchase powdered drink mixes in white plastic jars.

GET SET...

Cover one work area with wax paper and set out the cookies, icing, knives, and decorations. Cover another work area with newspapers and set out the craft materials. Ask children what things they would miss from home if they were in a distant place. Suggest things such as favorite foods, songs, people, and even pets. Explain that missionaries serving God in other parts of the world miss things from home, such as favorite cookies, and that kids can do something kind for them in this season of celebration. Read aloud Philippians 1:3-6, then briefly discuss missionaries' important jobs, why Jesus wants us to help missionaries, and ways we can support them.

Tell children you'll be making special springtime cookies and angel cookie jars to thank missionaries for their service to God and to let them know they're loved. Explain that the angel cookie jars will remind everyone how the angel rolled the stone from Jesus' tomb to let us know that Jesus is alive!

Go SERVE!

Form two teams: the cookie capers and the jolly jars. Have the cookie capers use icing, tiny candies, and sprinkled powdered sugar to decorate cookies. The jolly jars will make angel cookie jars by gluing excelsior hair to the jar lid. (If you like, add a ribbon halo.) Use paint or markers to add cute faces. Then glue wide lace around the jars for robes and tie ribbon bows at the necks. (Add buttons down the front of the jar for an extra decorative touch.)

Carefully fill each cookie jar with cookies, then add a note card with the words to Philippians 1:3 written on it. Your class may even wish to write thank-you notes to send along with the tasty treats. Box up the delicious goodies, then send them to missionaries your church or denomination sponsors.

These cute cookie gifts make wonderful service projects to present to seniors in care centers or to local homeless shelters. And for an extra loving touch, toss in a handful of candy conversation hearts!

CIRCLES of LOVE

Easter: Jesus died for our sins.

Service Scripture: Romans 5:8

GET READY...

This symbolic service project provides a way for kids to give to another class in your church and remind them that Christ loved them enough to die for them. You'll need a Bible, red sequins, tacky craft glue, red satin cord, a paper punch, fine-tipped permanent markers, scissors, and white poster board. You'll need to make several cross patterns for kids to trace and cut out of white poster board. Make the crosses about 3 inches long and 1 inch wide.

GET SET...

Gather kids and invite them to tell about the most wonderful or awesome gift they have ever received. Then read aloud Romans 5:8. Ask:

- **How was Jesus' death on the cross the most wonderful gift we've been given?**
- **What might have happened if Christ hadn't loved us enough to die for our sins?**
- **Why is it important to remind others of the sacrifice Jesus made for us?**

Remind kids that because of Christ's great love for us, he provided a way for our sins to be forgiven and a way for us to have eternal life. Explain that Easter is all about remembering Christ's sacrifice of love and celebrating the new life he brings us when we accept him as our Savior. Tell kids their service project today is to make wonderful crosses to remind the kids in another class of the gift of life and love Jesus gave to us through his death on the cross.

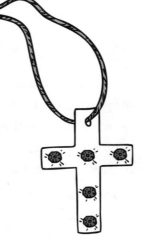

GO SERVE!

Have kids trace crosses on white poster board, then cut out the crosses. Use a paper punch to make holes at the tops of the crosses and thread a 16-inch length of red satin cord through each hole. Tie the ends of the cord to make a necklace.

Then explain that when Jesus died for us, he suffered five main wounds: two on his hands, two on his feet, and one in his side. Tell kids that some traditions maintain that when Mark took the gospel of Jesus to other lands and people, he used five circles with tiny dots to represent the five wounds of Jesus on the cross and to show that Jesus' love continues going around forever—just as a circle goes round and round. When people saw these symbols, it reminded them of how Jesus died for their sins. Have kids glue five red sequins to their crosses, then put tiny black dots in the holes of the sequins to make the five circles of Christ's love.

When the necklaces are dry, present them to the kids in another class and tell them what the crosses mean. Then lead them in a prayer thanking Jesus for his sacrifice of life and love. If there's time, let the kids in your class make their own circles of Christ's love necklaces to wear.

"CHILI" BUT WARM!

Community

Thanksgiving: Let's be thankful for those who help us!
Service Scripture: Psalm 100:4, 5

GET READY...

These edible thank-yous are as delicious to eat as they are fun to prepare! Say "thank you" to local firefighters for working to keep our holidays safe and sound. For each thanksgiving sack, you'll need four cans of chili with beans, two packages of Jiffy brand cornbread mix, a paper sack, and six self-adhesive labels (for file folders). You'll also need fine-tipped permanent markers.

GET SET...

Challenge kids to brainstorm all the community helpers we have to be thankful for, including police, highway patrol, city workers, the park department, and firefighters. Remind kids that these special workers labor during the holidays to keep us safe and secure. Tell kids your community service project will thank the firefighters who must miss being with their families during the holidays to keep our families safe.

GO SERVE!

For each thanksgiving sack, write the words: "Thanks for helping us in a (space)" on two labels and stick them just to the left of the word *Jiffy* on the cornbread mix. (You may need to cut off any extra label to make the words flow in a sentence.) Create labels for the chili cans that read: "Our hearts aren't (space) but warm with thanks!" Cut out the words "Our hearts aren't" and stick them just to the left of the word *Chili* on the cans. Then cut out the words "but warm with thanks!" and stick them to the right of the word *Chili* to make the sentence, "Our hearts aren't Chili but warm with thanks!"

Place the cans and boxes in brown paper sacks that you've decorated with thankful messages and colorful designs. You may want kids to write "Psalm 100:4, 5" on the sacks as a special expression of your thanks and God's love as well!

THANKS KERNELS

Family/Church

Thanksgiving: In all things, we give thanks.

Service Scripture: 1 Thessalonians 5:18

GET READY...

Want to get family, friends, and others thinking about thanks? Try this quick-n-easy service project anytime in November. You'll need a

As we have opportunity, let us do good to all people.

Bible, plastic wrap, plenty of candy corn, curling ribbon, scissors, and copies of the Care Card from the top of page 125.

GET SET...

Hand each child two pieces of candy corn and challenge kids to think of the two things they're most thankful for. Then have kids form pairs or trios and tell their partners what those two things are before nibbling their candies. Remind kids that God blesses us in so many ways, both big and small, and that we're to give thanks in all things! Read aloud 1 Thessalonians 5:18, then ask:

- ☙ **In what ways are God's provisions a demonstration of his love for us?**
- ☙ **Why is it important to give thanks in all things and not just for the big things God does?**

Explain that during this time of Thanksgiving, our thoughts turn to the many things we can give thanks for. Tell kids that this holiday service project revolves around getting people into an attitude of gratitude and to encourage them to think about thanks!

GO SERVE!

Have kids wrap three kernels of candy corn in plastic wrap, then tie curling ribbon around the packages. Tape a Care Card to each package, then distribute the packages to family members, friends, and even the entire congregation. Encourage others to think about thanks and then express their thanks to the Lord for all he lovingly gives and does for us!

A KERNEL OF THANKS, A BUSHEL, OR CRATE— EVERY BLESSING FROM GOD IS GLORIOUS AND GREAT!

"Give thanks in all circumstances"
(1 Thessalonians 5:18).

92

MiNi TREES

Christmas: We can spread God's ever-fresh love.

Service Scripture: John 15:12

GET READY...

You'll need sprigs of evergreen or other greenery, modeling dough, paper clips, gift wrap and bows, tape, fine-tipped markers, wrapped candy canes, construction paper, scissors, and empty containers such as plastic cups, small boxes, or cans. Check Christmas tree nurseries or flower shops for small branches of evergreen, holly, or other sturdy greenery.

GET SET...

Invite kids to tell about a time they were reminded of someone's love or how much someone cared for them. Remind kids that love is a growing thing and that when our love is based in Jesus' love, it stays fresh and lively forever—just like the evergreens we see at Christmas. Read John 15:12, then point out how important it is to remind others that we love and care for them. Ask:

- **How can it help or encourage others to know they're loved?**
- **In what ways can we show our love to others? demonstrate Jesus' love to others?**
- **How can love that is spread to others keep spreading?**

Explain that older adults can often feel lost, lonely, and forgotten, especially at Christmastime. Tell kids that seniors need to know that they're not forgotten, but loved, valued, and cared for! Explain that today you'll be making lovely evergreen decorations to remind people in a senior care center of yours and Jesus' special love!

Go SERVE!

Have kids use festive gift wrap and bows to decorate the cups, boxes, or cans. Then instruct kids to squish modeling dough into the

As we have opportunity, let us do good to all people.

bottoms of the containers. Gently poke branches of evergreen and holly into the modeling dough to make miniature "Christmas trees." Make small ornaments from construction paper and use partially unbent paper clips to hang them on the branches. Tape stars to the tops of the tiny trees. Make small construction-paper gift cards that having loving notes such as "I love you and so does Jesus!" written on them. Finally, poke one or two candy canes into the dough of each decoration for the recipient to enjoy along with all the Christmas love and cheer your mini trees will bring!

COOKIE CAPERS

Church/ Friends

Christmas: Jesus helps shoulder our loads.
Service Scripture: Matthew 11:28; Galatians 6:2

GET READY...

This cool cookie exchange will help take the cooking burden off of families and friends in this busy time of year. You'll need a Bible, plenty of canned icing and cans of squirty icing, candy sprinkles and tiny cinnamon candies, coconut, jam, plastic and paper plates, plastic wrap, trays or cookies sheets, powdered sugar, and a variety of prepared cookies, including fig bars, sugar cookies, butter cookie rings, sandwich cookies, and brownies.

GET SET...

Set up a cookie-decorating assembly line on a long table or two. Place cookies at one end, icing next, then candy sprinkles and other embellishments. Place the finished cookies on large trays or cookie sheets.

Read aloud Matthew 11:28 and Galatians 6:2. Then invite kids to tell how Jesus helps lessen our heavy loads, worries, and other burdens. Ask:

    ❻ **How does sharing work lessen the load for others?**

⚄ Why is it important to share the work load, especially at busy times such as Christmas?

Explain that Christmas is one of the busiest times of the year and that there's a way kids can all help share the work and lessen the load for moms and dads who want to do special Christmas cookie baking but can't find the time. Tell kids that they'll turn into pretend elves to help make beautiful treats to share and eat!

GO SERVE!

Have kids form two groups: icers to frost the cookies and embellishers to decorate the iced cookies. Invite kids to use the decorating suggestions below for the cookies—and be sure to let groups switch roles halfway through!

When you're finished making all the cookies, invite moms and dads to visit your cookie bazaar and each choose a half dozen cookies to take home and add to their own trays of goodies—or nibble with their kids right away! (Be sure to provide paper plates and plastic wrap.)

FIG-BAR BEAUTIES—Dust fig bars with a bit of powdered sugar, then use squirty icing to make three green holly leaves on each bar. Use a bit of icing as "glue" and stick on several tiny cinnamon candy "berries."

BUTTER RING WREATHS & HALOS—Spread green icing around the butter ring cookies, then glue on a few cinnamon berries. For a colorful variation, make Heavenly Halos by spreading yellow icing around the rings, then sprinkling them with yellow candy sugar.

SANDWICH COOKIE ORNAMENTS—Spread icing over the tops of sandwich cookies and decorate them as Christmas tree ornaments, using candy sprinkles and squirty icing.

MANGER COOKIES—Spread icing over the tops of sugar cookies, then sprinkle the icing with shredded coconut "hay." Finally, add a dollop of jam in the center as a reminder of Jesus' sweetness as he lay in the manger.

As we have opportunity, let us do good to all people.

SPECIAL NAME

Christmas: Jesus calls us by name!

Service Scripture: John 10:3

GET READY...

You'll need a Bible, empty egg cartons, scissors, glitter-glue pens (or glue and shake-on glitter), newspapers, and lots of Christmas tree ornament balls. Use the large, solid-colored satin or plastic Christmas balls to avoid breakage. Purchase the ornaments from a discount store and be sure you have a variety of festive colors! You may wish to purchase a box of inexpensive ornament hangers (like paper clips) to hand out with the finished decorations. Before beginning, cut apart the egg cups from the cartons. These will be used as drying stands for the ornaments and as carriers for recipients to cart home their special gifts. Decide in advance whether you will make personalized ornaments for everyone in church or another class. Purchase supplies and recruit teen helpers to match the number of ornaments you wish to provide.

GET SET...

Toss a Christmas ball around the room and challenge kids to repeat everyone's name. (New kids will certainly know everyone's name by the end of class!) Ask why we have names and if it is possible for anyone to know everyone's name in the entire world. Then read aloud John 10:3b. Ask:

- **Why is it neat that Jesus knows our names and even calls us by name?**
- **How does Jesus knowing our names demonstrate his love for us?**

Explain that Jesus knows our names because he cares for each one of us in special ways. And Jesus wants us to respond to his love and to obey him, so he calls us by name. Tell kids that this holiday season you'll help remind others that Jesus knows their names and loves them by personalizing Christmas ornaments with their names on them.

Go SERVE!

Set up a newspaper-covered table and provide kids with several names each. Have kids use glitter-glue pens to write the names, one per ornament. Tell kids they can add simple designs (if time permits), such as hearts, crosses, or stars. Place the finished personalized ornaments in egg cups but be sure the glitter glue doesn't touch the sides of the cups.

When the personalized gifts are dry, present them by visiting the appropriate classroom (or the congregation). Call out the names on the Christmas ornaments as you hand them out. What lovely reminders that our names are special to the Lord!

KINDNESS COUNTS

A class of third-graders in Iowa wanted to help feed the community while teaching them about growing good fruit. These kids visited local grocers for donations of apples, then handed out the apples with notes about planting the seeds and tending the young apple trees. Their challenge was for people to learn about caring and sharing through growing apple trees that would give more seeds to be planted. What a way to grow in God's grace!

SHEPHERDS' CANES

Christmas: Jesus is our good shepherd.

Service Scripture: Luke 2:8-20

Community/Church

GET READY...

You'll need red and white striped candy canes, white and red ribbon, scissors, a paper punch, markers or crayons, and photocopies of the Sweet Shepherd poem from page 126. Cut the ribbon into 6-inch lengths and be sure to have a poem for each candy cane you prepare.

GET SET...

Gather kids and invite them to tell everything they know about Jesus, including details about his birth, ministry, and death so we could have eternal life. Then ask:

- **How is Jesus' birth the best gift God has given us?**
- **Why is it a wonderful gift to tell someone about Jesus?**

Explain that sometimes during the Christmas hustle and bustle we forget what the reason for the season really is: the celebration of Jesus' life! Remind kids that one of the best ways to serve God is to tell others about Jesus' love, forgiveness, and the sacrifice he made so we could live forever.

Tell kids you can use something everyone sees at Christmastime to remember the reason for the season. Ask kids to guess what it might be, then explain that you will make special candy-cane reminders to hand out. (Decide beforehand whether you will hand these delicious treats out at church or possibly in a gift shop or a Christian bookstore. Be sure to ask permission if you plan on handing them out in public!)

GO SERVE!

Have kids cut out the Sweet Shepherd poems and color them (if there's time). You may even wish to have older children write a one-

As we have opportunity, let us do good to all people.

98

line greeting on the poems, such as "Jesus is our sweet reason for the season!" Punch a hole in the top of each poem and use red and white ribbons to tie the poems to candy canes. Finish with a prayer that asks God to help everyone the world over to stop their Christmas rush long enough to remember that Jesus is our sweet shepherd and that without Jesus, there would be no Christmas celebration!

SWEET POTPOURRI

Families/ Church

Christmas: Jesus' life was filled with sweet serving.

Service Scripture: Mark 10:45

GET READY...

Extend the Christmas season right into Easter with this unusual service project. During the weeks between Christmas and Easter, your kids will be making a delightful potpourri mix from evergreens and spices. At Easter, when the potpourri is complete, kids can present the project to their families to remind them of the sweet fragrance Jesus brings to our lives through his own life, death, and resurrection.

For this project, you'll need a cut Christmas tree or wreaths. Use a tree from one of the families at church after Christmas is over and snip off short sections of pine branches and needles so each child will have about 2 cups of pine. You'll also need plastic self-sealing bags, measuring spoons, and the following spices: cloves, cinnamon sticks, sea salt, and an orange for each child. For this week, you'll need the pine, plastic bags, oranges, and permanent markers.

GET SET...

Set out the materials and invite children to tell about Jesus' birth, death, and resurrection. Encourage them to tell ways that Jesus served us through each of these events or stages of his life. Read Mark 10:45, then ask:

As we have opportunity, let us do good to all people.

⬧ **How was Jesus' entire life an example of loving service to us?**

⬧ **In what ways can we model ourselves after Jesus and his serving nature?**

Explain that there are special events many churches celebrate between Christmas and Easter. Tell kids that Christmas is the celebration of Jesus' birth, that Epiphany is often celebrated as the time the wise men brought their gifts to Jesus, and that Easter is the time we observe and celebrate Jesus' death and joyous resurrection. Explain that the Bible tells us sweet fragrances symbolize things that are pleasing to God and that the sweetest "fragrance" of all was Jesus' life! Tell kids they'll be making special potpourri and will add new ingredients from now through Easter.

Go Serve!

Have kids form pairs or trios and hand each child an orange, a plastic bag, and 2 cups of pine to place in the bag. Instruct kids to peel their oranges and place the small pieces of rind in the bags with the pine. Write kids' names on the bags, then leave them unsealed in a dark place for two weeks. (Let kids eat their juicy oranges!)

At Epiphany (two weeks after Christmas), bring out the bags and add 1 tablespoon of ground cloves, 2 broken cinnamon sticks, and ⅓ cup of coarsely ground sea salt (available at health stores or cooking shops) to each bag. Explain how these ingredients symbolize the fragrant gifts the wise men brought to honor Jesus. Seal the bags loosely and place them in a dark closet for 6 to 8 weeks or until Easter Sunday. Bring the bags of potpourri out of the dark closet on Easter Sunday morning to symbolize Jesus' resurrection from the darkness of the tomb and death. The fragrant potpourri is ready for kids to take home to their families as sweet reminders of how Jesus' life and love were fragrant offerings to God and to us!

QUICK HOLIDAY HELPS

Here are plenty of quick and easy holiday ideas to make celebrations special, times memorable, and serving count! These ideas may be used with various holidays, or consider using them when you want to give someone a boost or create your own holiday *any* day!

PASTOR'S DAY

Want to say "thanks" and give a boost to your fearless leader? Then invent your own "Pastor's Day" celebration and consider serving the pastor, minister, or other church leaders a special meal in a quiet place after church. Provide a delicious turkey-and-tomato sandwich, chips, fruit cup, and cookie your class has prepared with love. Write quick notes of thanks and compile them into a booklet wrapped with a ribbon for the perfectly sweet "dessert"!

APRIL FOOLS' DAY

Give the gift of laughter by having kids bring in their favorite funny family photos and create fancy or funky frames for the special treasures. Use old jigsaw puzzle pieces or Sunday comics glued around cardboard frames. Wrap the pictures in colorful funny papers and have kids present the gifts to their families to place on the dining table to inspire memories, chats, and lots of laughter!

GROUNDHOG DAY

How many parents, grandparents, and kids love to see silhouettes of their loved ones? Host a silhouette-making day by setting up sheets of paper against a wall and shining lights on the profiles of participants. Trace the outlines, then cut them out of black construction paper and mount the silhouettes on white poster board. Shadows were never so sweet!

As we have opportunity, let us do good to all people.

NATIONAL DAY OF PRAYER

Celebrate the fact that God hears and answers our prayers with these delightful reminders. Photocopy the small poem on page 125 to hand out with pretty seashells kids have collected or made from paper or colorful modeling clay, such as Sculpy or Fimo brands.

As we hear the sea in each tiny shell,
So God hears our prayers
AND ANSWERS AS WELL!

ARBOR DAY

Celebrate Arbor Day by letting kids plant an evergreen bush or tree on church property. Have each child take a turn at digging, then set the plant in the ground and take turns covering the roots with soil and watering the new planting. Remind kids that "evergreen" means the plant is green and growing all year long—just as our faith in God grows and is alive!

MAY DAY

Make cute May baskets to hand to children in a local hospital. Create baskets from rolled cones of paper. Tape the cones to hold the sides in pointed basket shapes, then add goodies such as drawing pads, crayons, markers, and pencils. Have kids write cheery, encouraging notes and tuck them in the May baskets.

JOHNNY APPLESEED DAY

Shine a variety of apples with stems. Tie ribbons on the stems and tape notes to the ribbons that remind people that they are the apple of God's eye (Psalm 17:8). Present your nutritious service projects to a local food pantry, homeless shelter, or even the congregation some autumnlike Sunday morning!

QUICK ACTS OF KINDNESS

"MY FATHER WILL HONOR THE ONE WHO SERVES ME."

John 12:26

QUICK ACTS OF KINDNESS

Want your kids to get QUAK-ing? Then offer them the chance to use quick acts of kindness to serve others! (QUick Acts of Kindness = QUAK!) These are instant frown-busters guaranteed to lift spirits and put smiles on faces and hugs in hearts! Each of the QUAKs in this section can be completed in a few minutes but offers miles of smiles in return. Get kids thinking of serving God as a daily joy instead of a once-a-year drudge with these joy-filled service projects. If we're to pray and give thanks continually, we can surely strive to serve God and others continually, too!

i CARE COUPONS

You'll need a Bible, white or colored index cards, scissors, a stapler, markers, bingo daubers, a variety of stickers, and construction paper or old wallpaper books.

Special Note: You may want to make a sample coupn book so kids can see what a book looks like. These special coupons books make lovely Mother's or Father's Day gifts, too.

Set out the craft materials, then ask kids to form small groups and brainstorm special things to do for family members such as wash dishes, clean out the garage, mow the yard, or take Poochie for a walk. Ask everyone why serving our family members is as important as serving others. Ask a volunteer to read aloud 2 Peter 1:5-8, then briefly discuss how kindness, love, patience and self-control help families get along. Show

Good for one free dishwashing and A HUG!

kids your sample coupon book. Explain that today you'll be making cool little coupon books with coupons to give to family members.

Invite kids to design coupons that begin with the words "Good for one free..." or "This coupon entitles you to a..." Have kids design an "I care coupon" for each family member. Use markers, bingo daubers, and colorful stickers to decorate the coupons. Then let kids use construction paper or wallpaper samples to make neat covers. Staple the index-card coupons between the covers.

When the coupon booklets are complete, have kids take them home to present to their families. Challenge kids to keep the kindness coming even when the coupons are gone!

LOVE ABACUS

Make fun bead counters by putting five colored beads on a thin, plastic drinking straw or coffee stir stick. Put a small glob of florists' clay on each end to keep the beads on the rod. As kids work, explain that their families can use these cool counters to become aware of their own acts of kindness and serving. Each time someone in the family says or does something kind, encouraging, or loving, move a bead to the other side of the straw. Try to move all the beads to one side each day and back the next day. (You can give each bead a color code and write the code on small cards to go with the projects. Use this code as a sample: red = love; white = kindness; pink = a hug; and so on.)

HANDLE WITH CARE!

Purchase, or ask a mail center for a donation of "Handle With Care" stickers and hand each person five of the self-adhesive labels and a fine-tipped marker. Under the words *Handle With Care,* have kids write, "God is there!" Then invite kids to use colorful markers to decorate the edges of the stickers. Tell kids that these are everyday reminders that hearts, dreams, faith, and feelings must be treated kindly and nurtured. Remind kids that "God is there" helping us to be kind and loving to others! Hand out the stickers to friends and family members who may need a boost of loving care and kindness as well as a reminder that God is always with them!

SWEET LIPS

Make sweet lip balm to remind church members how sweet God's Word is on our lips (Psalm 119:103). In a bowl, mix petroleum jelly and flavor extracts. Flavors might include strawberry, coconut, cherry, or even bubble gum! Fill small tins, tiny vials, or other miniature containers with your flavored lip balm. Attach a card with the words to Psalm 119:103 written on it, then distribute your sweet reminders to church members as everyday reminders of the sweetness of God's Word on our lips!

WORTH A MILLION!

Give thanks for church volunteers and helpers with this cute idea. Purchase small bags of gold chocolate coins or $100,000 brand candy bars. Attach notes of thanks that begin with "You're Worth a Million!" These clever thank-yous are appreciated anytime as a boost and encouragement for serving others. (Consider giving these bodacious bars to your own class in recognition of their serving savvy!)

STICKY SMILES

These everyday notes do wonders in bringing smiles, warmth, and delight to anyone who finds them! Hand each child a small pad of self-adhesive notes and a fine-tipped marker or pen. Let kids work in pairs or trios to decorate the first twelve notes with smiles, tiny pictures, and encouraging words and messages. As kids work, explain that the purpose of this project is to leave these cheery greetings and smile-makers for family members, school friends, and anyone else who needs a surprise lift! The notes can be attached to mirrors, lockers, lunch bags, car dashboards, and a host of other interesting places. Encourage kids to create more memorable messages when they have only a few designs left and challenge them to completely use up their sticky note pads over the next month. Just think of all the smiles kids will inspire!

FUN CLIPS

This cool project is guaranteed to bring smiles to families. Have kids choose hinge-style clothespins and use fine-tipped permanent markers to write "Serve one another in love" on one side and "Galatians 5:13" on the other. Then decorate the clips using glitter glue and markers. Explain that one family member clips the clothespin someplace in the house. When someone finds the clip, he or she must serve another family member in some way, such as doing a chore, saying something kind, or even drawing a picture for the person. After serving, clip the clothespin in a new place for someone else to find.

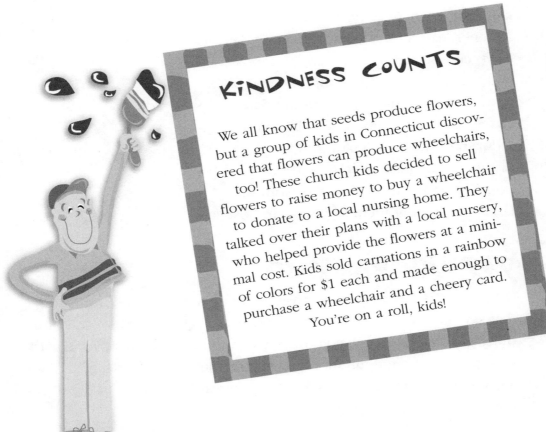

KINDNESS COUNTS

We all know that seeds produce flowers, but a group of kids in Connecticut discovered that flowers can produce wheelchairs, too! These church kids decided to sell flowers to raise money to buy a wheelchair to donate to a local nursing home. They talked over their plans with a local nursery, who helped provide the flowers at a minimal cost. Kids sold carnations in a rainbow of colors for $1 each and made enough to purchase a wheelchair and a cheery card. You're on a roll, kids!

BIRTHDAY JEWELS

Kids will enjoy making these cool jewels to give to other kids on their birthdays. Have kids use patterns to cut out stars and hearts from poster board. Punch holes in the tops of the shapes and thread fishing line or yarn through them to make necklaces. On the backs of the shapes, write the name of a month, then on the front glue a plastic jewel that coordinates to that month's birthstone (for example, blue for December's aquamarine). Make many shapes for each month, then as someone's birthday arrives, present him with a special birthstone birthday greeting!

(For color suggestions, use the following: January—red; February—purple; March—light blue; April—clear; May—dark green; June—light blue; July—red; August—light green; September—blue; October—yellow; November—light blue; December—blue.)

CANDY BOUQUETS

These tasty blossoms make every day special! For each flower, have kids take a length of florists' wire and use florists' tape to secure several paper leaves to the flower "stem."

Next, choose a piece of wrapped candy and use florists' tape to wrap one end of the candy paper to the end of the wire as the "blossom." Have each child make a dozen of these delightful flowers to distribute to family, friends, and neighbors—or tie them into bunches with ribbons and present them to people in hospitals or care centers.

POP-UP PROJECT

Use the cool pop-up pattern on the bottom of page 127 for cards that say "Get Well!" "Thank You!" "Welcome!" "Jesus Loves You!" or any other greeting or message you can create. Simply photocopy the card pattern on stiff paper and let kids cut out the cards and decorate them according to your service theme. Fold the card according to the directions, and your pop-up greetings are complete!

SERVING SPIRALS

Help kids teach others about the way serving spirals outward to reach more and more people. Review the Serving Spiral with God always at the center of serving, then moving outward to touch family, friends, church, community, and the world. Hand each child six wrapped swirly mint candies. Ask kids to identify the spirals of serving, with God always at the center. Then challenge kids to hand out five mints as they remind others about serving God and others in many ways.

(A wonderful variation of this idea is to assemble Serving Spiral trees to set in doctors' offices for severely ill patients who might need a sweet lift. Simply pin the candy wrappers to Styrofoam cones and place a card at the top of each tree that says, "A sweet lift for you!")

FUZZY FRIENDS

These cute and cuddly pompon friends will remind others that God's warmth and love is with them wherever they go! Purchase several bags of googly eyes and colorful, medium-sized pompons. Plan on having each child make at least three fuzzy friends: one to keep and two to give away. You'll also need craft felt, tacky craft glue, and scissors. Cut funny feet from craft felt and glue them to the bottom of a pompon ball. Glue on a set of googly eyes. If kids are really creative, suggest felt facial features and other accessories, such as glasses, hair, hats, buttons, earmuffs, or even tiny Bibles. Have kids think of who they could give their warm reminders of God's warm love to, then encourage kids to present their fuzzy friends as they remind their human friends about God's abiding love.

CROWNED JEWELS

Let your kids serve preschoolers in church by making them fancy crowns and teaching the younger children that serving others brings great treasures of love. Pick up crowns from restaurants who may be giving them away or make crowns from yellow poster board. (You may wish to wait to size the crowns until you present them to the younger children. Simply fit the crowns to the preschoolers' heads and tape the ends for a custom fit!) Embellish the crowns with sequins, glitter glue, and plastic jewels. Write "Serving is a treasure!" on the backs of the crowns.

Have your kids explain about serving: that when we serve others, we serve God and that serving makes us feel awesome inside and out! Tell preschoolers that the treasures on their crowns stand for the treasures of love, help, and kindness that we bring to others when we serve them every day.

SPIN-A-CHORE

Let kids experience "walking in someone else's shoes" with this fun service project. Have kids use markers to divide paper plates into six pie wedges. Have kids write six chores that are typically done by others, such as washing dishes, doing yard work, emptying the trash, dusting, and folding laundry. Then cut 2-by-½-inch rectangles from poster board or old folders. Clip the tips to make pointing arrows and use a hole punch to make holes in the straight ends of the arrows. Attach the arrows to the centers of the paper plates so the arrows spin when flicked. On the backs of the Spin-a-Chore plates, have kids write Galatians 5:13 as a reminder that when we serve others, we're also serving God! Tell kids to spin the arrow each day for the next two weeks and serve someone in the family by taking over the chore indicated. Kids can even encourage other family members to each take a spin on the chore wheel and have a bit of fun sharing their everyday work!

CLEANING CREWS

Let kids form pairs and use permanent markers to decorate and personalize small buckets. Encourage kids to create a cleaning-crew name for each set of partners. (Form one or two trios if necessary.) When the buckets are finished, have kids fold several paper towels to place in their buckets along with a sponge, a small spritz bottle filled with water and vinegar to use as a nontoxic cleaning compound, and a soft, flannel cloth. Whenever you want to give a quick bit of service, call out the cleaning crews and let them go to work! Consider having crews clean the church library once a month, wash tables or desks, polish doorknobs, clean floorboards, or dust hallway corners and light switch plates. Kids will love their responsibilities, and these small cleaning jobs are usually the most overlooked—and greatly appreciated!

HAPPY-GRAMS

This quick-n-easy service project will bring smiles to the most stubborn lips! Let kids use cans of squirty icing to decorate small vanilla cookies or sandwich cookies. Place the happy cookies on large trays or cookie sheets and offer them to the congregation as they're leaving church services. Tell kids to smile as they offer their treats and to remind others that serving God makes us happy! Consider using this idea to raise money for Operation Smile, which helps children who have been burned or scarred keep smiling. (See Service Directory.)

WALLET CARDS

Photocopy the cards on page 126 on stiff paper. Make copies for each child and the members in her family. Invite kids to color the cards with markers, then write short messages of encouragement or love on the backs of the cards.

Carefully cover the completed cards with clear, self-adhesive paper for durability. Explain that these wallet cards can be slipped into billfolds or wallets and be carried with family members as reminders of love and support.

Wherever you go,
Whatever you do,
Always remember
I'm thinking of you!

Joshua 1:9

POSTCARD PALS

Ask the adults in a retirement center (or even seniors in your congregation) if they would like to write notes back and forth with kids in your class and be Postcard Pals. (Chances are, you'll have many lonely or bored seniors jump at this delightful prospect!) Have kids work either alone or in pairs to correspond with their Postcard Pals. Purchase or make a stack of postcards that kids can use to write their notes and be sure to provide plenty of postage stamps. Encourage Postcard Pals to exchange a simple note once a week for the next six months. Remind kids that when we give of our time and ourselves, it is more precious than giving the richest treasures in the world!

FLASH CARDS

Ask kids to write out their two favorite Bible verses about particular themes, such as love, fear, anger, forgiveness, or serving. (Let kids use a concordance or have them thumb through the New Testament for their verses.) Write the verses on index-card halves, then tape the cards to sheets of paper (you will have many cards per page). Photocopy the pages on stiff paper and let the kids cut out the cards. Have each child slide a set of cards in an envelope to take home. Challenge kids to use the cards as flash cards to help their family members learn God's Word. Set a goal of learning one card each week and reviewing every previously learned verse each week as well.

SHARE-A-PRAYER GARLAND

This simple project will remind others to give thanks for the everyday blessings God provides. Have each child make a list of seven everyday things he is thankful for, such as food, light, love, flowers, or friends. Then have kids cut construction-paper shapes to represent those things; for example, a lamp for light or a heart for love. Have kids tape the shapes to 3-foot lengths of thick yarn or wide ribbon and place the garlands in envelopes. Hand out the envelopes to the members of the youth group, adult Sunday school, or another class of kids and explain that these garlands can be hung on the wall as reminders of the everyday things we can thank God for. Encourage the recipients to thank God each day for one of the blessings represented on the garland.

WONDERFUL WATER

Kids will enjoy making the cups that go along with this unique Sunday service idea. Have kids get in pairs or trios and be sure there is a group assigned to every teacher or leader in your church. Have each group use glitter-glue pens and paint pens to personalize a cup for their assigned church helper. Beginning the next week, have partners be in charge of filling the cup with cold water before classes or sermons begin and present their gift of cool water to the assigned recipient. After the class or the sermon, have the partners quickly wash the cup and store it away to use next week. Challenge kids to serve in this way for the remainder of the year. Kids will discover that even a small act of kindness is so greatly appreciated!

ZIPPER-DEE-DOO-DA!

This fanciful service project will remind kids that "God is in control, so don't worry!" Plan on having each child make two of these cool items: one to wear and one to share with someone in another class. (Be sure you make enough zipper pulls to present to all the kids in another classroom!) Have kids use colorful, quick-dry craft clay and design clay characters of things in God's control. Suggestions for designs and shapes might include the earth, a tree or flower, a person or face, a mountain, a star, or a heart. Make the clay figures about 2 inches tall and slide a paper clip one third of the way into the top of each figure. Dry the figures in a warm (250 degree) oven for 10 minutes (or according to package instructions), then present your colorful figures to the kids in another class to wear on jacket or backpack zippers as reminders that God controls everything in the world and that we can trust his power every day!

RECORD A MESSAGE

This service project may take a few minutes but can be enjoyed every day in a snap! Have kids find and write down their favorite Bible verses. These can be Scripture verses they've been working to memorize, verses from favorite Bible stories, or thematic verses such as ones about loving others, forgiveness, or our salvation through Jesus. Have kids practice reading their verses aloud, then record the verses as they're read aloud on cassette tape. Make copies for each child to take home and play for family members. Suggest playing one verse a day after dinner and discussing the meaning of the verse with others in the family.

For a variation, record kids reading the Beatitudes (Matthew 5:3-10), the Golden Rule (Matthew 7:12), and Psalm 23.

GIFT OF ME!

Invite kids to design three coupons that entitle the recipients to 30 minutes of one-on-one time with a child. Decorate the coupons with fanciful designs and word the coupons something like this: "This coupon entitles you to 30 MINUTES with me!" As kids work, remind them that one of the best gifts we can give someone is the gift of time and ourselves. Point out that serving others involves giving them our time, which is how we serve God, too! Suggestions for what to do with 30 minutes of time? Kids can offer to do chores, rake yards, read a story to a sibling, run a quick errand, clean the garage, or simply spend a bit of time chatting and bringing the gift of laughter to someone!

ERASABLE BOOKMARKS

These clever bookmarks will serve as handy reminders each day of what you've been learning in the Bible! Have kids cut 8-by-3-inch lengths of colorful poster board. Glue flat, dried flowers, clover, leaves, or stickers to the ends of the bookmarks. In the centers, write the days of the week. List Monday through Thursday on one side of the bookmarks and Friday through Sunday on the other side. Then laminate the bookmarks or cover them with clear, self-adhesive paper. Finally, punch a hole at one end of the bookmark, thread a ribbon through the hole, and tie the ribbon in place. Have kids present these projects to the youth group to encourage them to read the Bible every day and to list the sections they read each day on their bookmarks. Instruct the youth group to use crayons or dry-erase pens to write on the bookmarks. (You could hand them out with the bookmarks as a bonus to your special project!) At the end of the week, the youth group can see how much of God's precious Word they have enjoyed! The bookmarks can then be erased and used again and again.

CHEF'S DAY OFF

Everyday cooking can be a grind for many parents, so why not serve them by giving them the day off? Let kids brainstorm simple recipes for sandwiches, snacks, salads, and other nutritious dishes that require little or no cooking. (Toast and some microwave soups would work well.) Then write the recipes on index cards and make copies of the cards so each child can take home a recipe-card box full of tasty treats and "good-to-eats"!

BUBBLE BLESSINGS

Praising God with joy and prayers is a great way to serve our heavenly Father. Let kids make special bubbles to send skyward with their prayers and thanksgiving for all God gives and does for us. Help kids mix bubble solution with a ratio of 3 cups water to 1 cup liquid dish soap and 1 tablespoon white corn syrup. (The corn syrup will help the bubbles keep their shape and last longer!) If the solution is weak or the bubbles burst easily, add a bit more soap. Make bubble blowers from bent twist-tie wires or chenille wires. If you want, use empty spools and dip the ends in, then blow away! As each bubble ascends, have kids give a word of thanks for a particular blessing or offer a prayer request. End with a grand finale and blow bubbles of praise and joy heavenward!

BREAKFAST FOR THE BIRDS

Serve a bit of outdoor kindness by feeding the birds in the church yard. (If you have an inner-city church, you may wish to visit a nearby park or garden.) Hand each child a plastic sandwich bag filled with ½ cup of birdseed, unsalted sunflower seeds, popped popcorn, or cracker bits. Before spreading your offerings around, read aloud Psalm 84:1-4, then remind kids that all of God's creation honors him and wants to be near him. Point out that when we serve with kindness in our hearts, we move closer to God. Sprinkle the birdseed around, then offer a prayer thanking God for ways to bring us closer to him. Read aloud Psalm 84:1-4 once again. (You may wish to send another small bag of birdseed home with kids to serve to the birds in their yards.)

My Father will honor the one who serves me.

SAMARITAN BANDAGES

Kids will love decorating special bandages to hand to those who are sick, sad, or hurt. Have plenty of various shapes and sizes of plastic bandages for kids to decorate and plan on letting each child make six bandages to take home. Use fine-tipped permanent markers to draw happy faces, flowers, hearts, stars, and other cheerful designs on the bandages. You may wish to write the references for Scripture verses such as Ezekiel 34:16 on some of the bandages. Have kids hand their projects to people who could use a smile, a lift, or a warm bandage for their hearts!

FRUIT OF SERVICE

This final service project is a sweet, tender one that reminds us of the power and preciousness of serving others and God. Photocopy on pastel paper the poem on page 127 by Mother Teresa. Have kids cut out the poems and tie them into scrolls with ribbons or rubber bands. Attach the scrolls to pieces of fruit such as apples (with stems). Plan on presenting the apples to the entire congregation and perhaps coordinate this service project with a sermon about being God's good fruit.

Service Directory

Following are a few places and organizations mentioned in the preceding pages. Check the World Wide Web for many more listings that offer services and help for people the world over!

CROP: Christian Rural Overseas Program
(Helps feed hungry people in third-world countries)
c/o Church World Service
28606 Phillips Street
P.O. Box 968
Elkhart, IN 46515
1-888-297-2767
www.churchworldservice.org/crop.html

OPERATION SMILE
(Helps kids around the world with burns or other scars to keep smiling)
6435 Tidewater Drive
Norfolk, VA 23509
757-321-7645
www.operationsmile.org

SAMARITAN'S PURSE
(Helps people around the world through hot-meals programs, Bibles and other Christian literature, and a host of other services)
P.O. Box 3000
Boone, NC 28607-3000
828-262-1980
www.samaritan.org

HABITAT FOR HUMANITY
(Helps build houses for needy families throughout the world)
Contact your local affiliate or the international headquarters.
Partner Service Center
Habitat for Humanity International

121 Habitat Street
Americus, GA 31709
1-800-422-4828
www.habitat.org

AMERICAN RED CROSS

(Provides relief to victims of storms, fire, and other natural disasters)
Contact your local branch or the national office.
Attn: Public Inquiry Office
11th Floor
1621 N. Kent Street
Arlington, VA 22209
1-703-248-4222
www.redcross.org

HEIFER PROJECT INTERNATIONAL

(Provides farm animals for needy villages around the world)
P.O. Box 808
Little Rock, AR 72203
1-800-422-0474
www.heifer.org

WORLD VISION

(Helps to feed, clothe, and educate children around the world)
U.S. Headquarters
World Vision Inc.
34834 Weyerhaeuser Way South
Federal Way, WA 98001
1-253-815-1000
www.worldvision.org

ORIENTAL TRADING COMPANY

(Catalogs offering big discounts for bulk gift items; contains Christian items for kids and adults)
P.O. Box 3407
Omaha, NE 68103-0407
1-800-246-8400
www.oriental.com or www.teachercentral.com

Your windows are clean, and oh what a view;
Jesus' love and forgiveness makes us sparkle like new!

"Therefore, if anyone is in Christ, he is a new creation; the old has gone, the new has come!" 2 Corinthians 5:17

Your windows are clean, and oh what a view;
Jesus' love and forgiveness makes us sparkle like new!

"Therefore, if anyone is in Christ, he is a new creation; the old has gone, the new has come!" 2 Corinthians 5:17

GOD HAS LOVED YOU FROM THE START— HERE'S SOMETHING ELSE TO WARM YOUR HEART!

Mix 2 spoonfuls in a cup of hot water or 1 spoonful in hot coffee.

"Be devoted to one another in brotherly love. Honor one another above yourselves." Romans 12:10

GOD HAS LOVED YOU FROM THE START— HERE'S SOMETHING ELSE TO WARM YOUR HEART!

Mix 2 spoonfuls in a cup of hot water or 1 spoonful in hot coffee.

"Be devoted to one another in brotherly love. Honor one another above yourselves." Romans 12:10

THANKS! THANKS!

Thanks for being a real lifesaver
Who loves and serves our real life Savior!
Philippians 1:3, 4

THANKS! THANKS!

THANKS! THANKS!

Thanks for being a real lifesaver
Who loves and serves our real life Savior!
Philippians 1:3, 4

THANKS! THANKS!

This sack is filled with good things for you—

We fill up with love when we serve others, too.

So help and love and show that you care,

And the world will be filled with love every-

where!

This sack is filled with good things for you—

We fill up with love when we serve others, too.

So help and love and show that you care,

And the world will be filled with love every-

where!

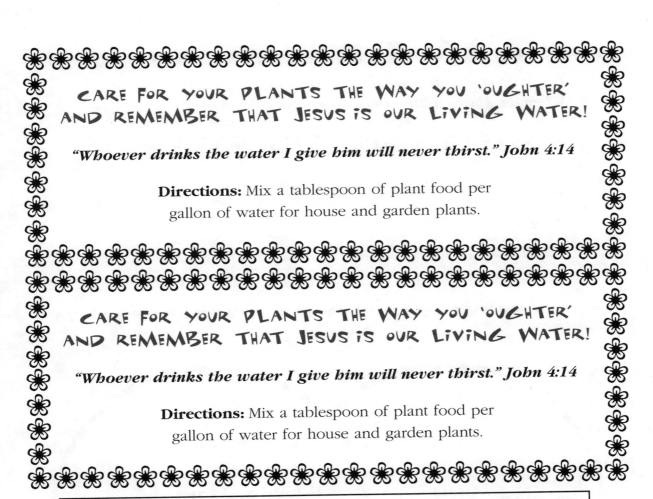

CARE FOR YOUR PLANTS THE WAY YOU 'OUGHTER' AND REMEMBER THAT JESUS IS OUR LIVING WATER!

"Whoever drinks the water I give him will never thirst." John 4:14

Directions: Mix a tablespoon of plant food per gallon of water for house and garden plants.

CARE FOR YOUR PLANTS THE WAY YOU 'OUGHTER' AND REMEMBER THAT JESUS IS OUR LIVING WATER!

"Whoever drinks the water I give him will never thirst." John 4:14

Directions: Mix a tablespoon of plant food per gallon of water for house and garden plants.

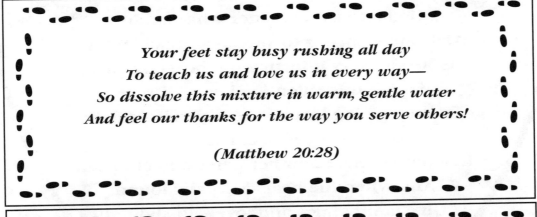

Your feet stay busy rushing all day
To teach us and love us in every way—
So dissolve this mixture in warm, gentle water
And feel our thanks for the way you serve others!

(Matthew 20:28)

Your feet stay busy rushing all day
To teach us and love us in every way—
So dissolve this mixture in warm, gentle water
And feel our thanks for the way you serve others!

(Matthew 20:28)

Tea for two or three or four—
When we share with others, love multiplies more!

COME TO OUR TEA PARTY!

WHEN:

WHERE:

COST: $1 or 2 cans of food (All proceeds and donations will go to a local food pantry!)

Hide-n-Seek Valentine

God's love for us is kind and true;
He loves us no matter what we do.
And God wants us to spread wonderful love
As he showers it forth from heaven above!
So use this Valentine heart all year
To keep giving love to those you hold dear.
Hide this heart like Hide-n-Seek
In a place where another person might peek.
And when the heart is finally found,
Give family hugs and love will abound!

"Love one another, for
love comes from God."
1 John 4:7

WE MAY EAT TiN CANS, SHOES, AND WEEDS— BUT WE ALSO PROVIDE FOR LOTS OF NEEDS!

Congratulations! You've just helped purchase a goat for a needy village!

In your honor, a portion of the goat's name will be:

_____

Thank you for your present of love—

and the gift of a goat!

"God loves a cheerful giver." 2 Corinthians 9:7

WE MAY EAT TiN CANS, SHOES, AND WEEDS— BUT WE ALSO PROVIDE FOR LOTS OF NEEDS!

Congratulations! You've just helped purchase a goat for a needy village!

In your honor, a portion of the goat's name will be:

_____

Thank you for your present of love—

and the gift of a goat!

"God loves a cheerful giver." 2 Corinthians 9:7

Welcome to _____

SUNDAY	MONDAY	TUESDAY	WEDNESDAY	THURSDAY	FRIDAY	SATURDAY
Pray for peace in your town, state, and country.				Do a kind deed for someone in your family!		
		Pray for someone at school or work.				Jot an encouraging note for someone in your family.
Read a favorite Bible verse to a friend.					Pray for people in another country to know Jesus.	
	Share something you have with someone today.		Make a friend smile or laugh today!			

A KERNEL OF THANKS,
A BUSHEL, OR CRATE—
EVERY BLESSING FROM GOD
IS GLORIOUS AND GREAT!

"Give thanks in all circumstances."
1 Thessalonians 5:18

A KERNEL OF THANKS,
A BUSHEL, OR CRATE—
EVERY BLESSING FROM GOD
IS GLORIOUS AND GREAT!

"Give thanks in all circumstances."
1 Thessalonians 5:18

A KERNEL OF THANKS,
A BUSHEL, OR CRATE—
EVERY BLESSING FROM GOD
IS GLORIOUS AND GREAT!

"Give thanks in all circumstances."
1 Thessalonians 5:18

A KERNEL OF THANKS,
A BUSHEL, OR CRATE—
EVERY BLESSING FROM GOD
IS GLORIOUS AND GREAT!

"Give thanks in all circumstances."
1 Thessalonians 5:18

As we hear the sea in each tiny shell,
So God hears our prayers
AND ANSWERS AS WELL!

As we hear the sea in each tiny shell,
So God hears our prayers
AND ANSWERS AS WELL!

SWEET SHEPHERD

An old candymaker made a sweet gift
To tell others of Jesus and give them a lift.
"This candy must be white and brightly a-glow,
For Jesus was pure as the new-fallen snow.
It must be rock hard," said the man with a nod,
"To show Jesus is our rock-solid promise from God!
I'll add a few stripes that are bright, rosy red
As his love and blood that for us were shed.
Finally I'll shape it to stand for his name—
And turned upside down, it's a sweet shepherd's cane!"
So whenever you see a bright candy cane,
It stands for our Savior and his sweet, precious name!

The fruit of silence is prayer—
The fruit of prayer is faith—
The fruit of faith is love—
The fruit of love is service—
The fruit of service is peace.

—Mother Teresa

The fruit of silence is prayer—
The fruit of prayer is faith—
The fruit of faith is love—
The fruit of love is service—
The fruit of service is peace.

—Mother Teresa

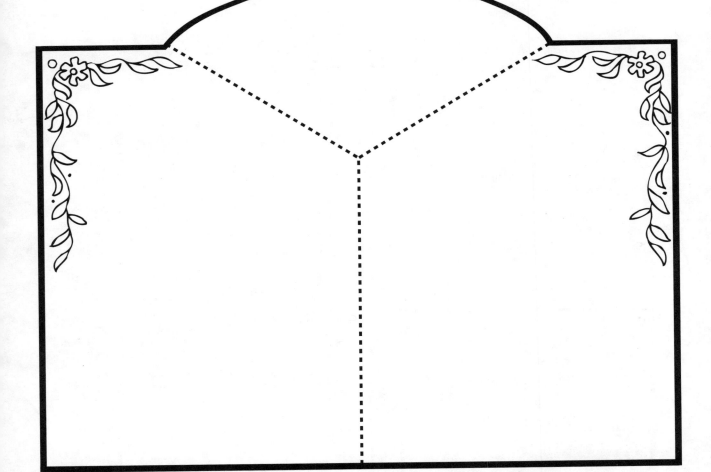